C-1766   CAREER EXAMINATION SERIES

This is your
PASSBOOK for...

Supervising Special Officer

Test Preparation Study Guide
Questions & Answers

COPYRIGHT NOTICE

This book is SOLELY intended for, is sold ONLY to, and its use is RESTRICTED to individual, bona fide applicants or candidates who qualify by virtue of having seriously filed applications for appropriate license, certificate, professional and/or promotional advancement, higher school matriculation, scholarship, or other legitimate requirements of education and/or governmental authorities.

This book is NOT intended for use, class instruction, tutoring, training, duplication, copying, reprinting, excerption, or adaptation, etc., by:

1) Other publishers
2) Proprietors and/or Instructors of "Coaching" and/or Preparatory Courses
3) Personnel and/or Training Divisions of commercial, industrial, and governmental organizations
4) Schools, colleges, or universities and/or their departments and staffs, including teachers and other personnel
5) Testing Agencies or Bureaus
6) Study groups which seek by the purchase of a single volume to copy and/or duplicate and/or adapt this material for use by the group as a whole without having purchased individual volumes for each of the members of the group
7) Et al.

Such persons would be in violation of appropriate Federal and State statutes.

PROVISION OF LICENSING AGREEMENTS – Recognized educational, commercial, industrial, and governmental institutions and organizations, and others legitimately engaged in educational pursuits, including training, testing, and measurement activities, may address request for a licensing agreement to the copyright owners, who will determine whether, and under what conditions, including fees and charges, the materials in this book may be used them. In other words, a licensing facility exists for the legitimate use of the material in this book on other than an individual basis. However, it is asseverated and affirmed here that the material in this book CANNOT be used without the receipt of the express permission of such a licensing agreement from the Publishers. Inquiries re licensing should be addressed to the company, attention rights and permissions department.

All rights reserved, including the right of reproduction in whole or in part, in any form or by any means, electronic or mechanical, including photocopying, recording, or by any information storage and retrieval system, without permission in writing from the Publisher.

Copyright © 2024 by
National Learning Corporation

212 Michael Drive, Syosset, NY 11791
(516) 921-8888 • www.passbooks.com
E-mail: info@passbooks.com

PASSBOOK® SERIES

THE *PASSBOOK® SERIES* has been created to prepare applicants and candidates for the ultimate academic battlefield – the examination room.

At some time in our lives, each and every one of us may be required to take an examination – for validation, matriculation, admission, qualification, registration, certification, or licensure.

Based on the assumption that every applicant or candidate has met the basic formal educational standards, has taken the required number of courses, and read the necessary texts, the *PASSBOOK® SERIES* furnishes the one special preparation which may assure passing with confidence, instead of failing with insecurity. Examination questions – together with answers – are furnished as the basic vehicle for study so that the mysteries of the examination and its compounding difficulties may be eliminated or diminished by a sure method.

This book is meant to help you pass your examination provided that you qualify and are serious in your objective.

The entire field is reviewed through the huge store of content information which is succinctly presented through a provocative and challenging approach – the question-and-answer method.

A climate of success is established by furnishing the correct answers at the end of each test.

You soon learn to recognize types of questions, forms of questions, and patterns of questioning. You may even begin to anticipate expected outcomes.

You perceive that many questions are repeated or adapted so that you can gain acute insights, which may enable you to score many sure points.

You learn how to confront new questions, or types of questions, and to attack them confidently and work out the correct answers.

You note objectives and emphases, and recognize pitfalls and dangers, so that you may make positive educational adjustments.

Moreover, you are kept fully informed in relation to new concepts, methods, practices, and directions in the field.

You discover that you are actually taking the examination all the time: you are preparing for the examination by "taking" an examination, not by reading extraneous and/or supererogatory textbooks.

In short, this PASSBOOK®, used directedly, should be an important factor in helping you to pass your test.

SUPERVISING SPECIAL OFFICER

DUTIES:
Supervising Special Officers, under general supervision, direct a unit of security personnel on a specific tour of duty in an assigned area. They supervise and evaluate work performance of subordinates, which may include contract guards; prepare, complete and/or review records, logs, and reports regarding patrols, demonstrations, arrests and other incidents relating to safety and security; interpret and enforce policy directives from higher authorities; counsel, train, and correct subordinates; plan and coordinate assignments of staff and equipment; respond to emergency situations; conduct roll call; inspect office, posts, and assigned work areas; may work in a secure detention facility; may appear in court and/or assist other law enforcement agencies on assault or arrest cases, as needed; may operate a motor vehicle while performing patrol duties; and perform related work.

THE TEST:
The multiple-choice test may include questions on the following areas: monitoring, evaluating, and correcting subordinates' performance; ensuring that subordinates comply with current safety and security procedures; completing and reviewing routine and administrative paperwork including forms, reports and logs; applying given general rules to particular situations; analyzing situations and deciding upon effective solutions; responding to emergency situations; communicating through written correspondence; interacting with subordinates, superiors, and the general public; conducting roll call; inspecting officers, posts, and assigned work areas; and appearing in court and/or assisting other law enforcement agencies on assault or arrest cases.

The test will include questions which may require the use of any of the following abilities:

1. **Planning and Organizing** - Establishing a method of execution to accomplish a specific goal over an extended period of time; determining appropriate assignments and allocation of resources. A Supervising Special Officer might use this ability when planning coverage for a special event.
2. **Innovation** - Developing new ideas and answers to work-related problems using creativity and alternative thinking A Supervising Special Officer might use this ability to develop new strategies.
3. **Management of Material Resources** - Obtaining and seeing to the appropriate use of equipment, facilities, and materials needed to do certain work; managing the things needed for work to be accomplished. A Supervising Special Officer might use this ability when designing feedback systems to make sure that assigned work was actually completed by subordinates.
4. **Management of Personnel Resources** - Motivating, developing, and directing people as they work, identifying the best people for the job; managing employees needed to accomplish tasks. A Supervising Special Officer might use this ability when assigning research, writing, statistical work, or investigations to appropriate subordinates.
5. **Monitoring** - Monitoring/assessing performance of oneself, other individuals or organizations to make improvements or take corrective action; overseeing the quality of performance. A Supervising Special Officer might use this ability to decide which problems should be given greatest priority and commitment of resources.

6. **Written Comprehension** - Understanding the information and ideas presented in written sentences and paragraphs in work-related documents. A Supervising Special Officer might use this ability to review narrative reports.
7. **Written Expression** - Appropriately communicating information and ideas in written words and sentences the intended audience will understand. A Supervising Special Officer might use this ability when preparing reports to management.
8. **Coaching and Mentoring** - Identifying the developmental needs of others and coaching, mentoring, or otherwise help others to improve their knowledge and skills. A Supervising Special Officer might use this ability to act as a exemplary role model, embodying and expecting the highest professional standards.
9. **Teamwork** - Developing a mutual trust and cooperation while working together toward the accomplishment of a common goal or outcome. A Supervising Special Officer might use this ability when planning coverage for a special event.
10. **Integrity** - Acting in an honest and ethical manner. A Supervising Special Officer might use this ability to function effectively as a leader, being neither too informal, nor too distant, and conveying a sense of professionalism and fairness.
11. **Updating and Using Relevant Knowledge** - Keeping up-to-date technically and applying new knowledge to the job. A Supervising Special Officer might use this ability when dealing with radio messages, verbal and written communication that use special terminology.

INTRODUCTION

This test guide provides a general description of the most common subject areas which will be tested and an explanation of the different types of questions you may see on the test.

Not all subject areas tested in the Safety and Security Series are covered in this test guide. The Examination Announcement will list the subject areas that will be included on the particular test you will be taking. Some of these subject areas may not be covered in this test guide.

The most common subject areas included in the Safety and Security Series are:

1. **APPLYING WRITTEN INFORMATION IN A SAFETY AND SECURITY SETTING:** These questions evaluate your ability to read, interpret and apply rules, regulations, directions, written narratives and other related material. You will be required to read a set of information and to appropriately apply the information to situations similar to those typically experienced in a public safety and security service setting. All information needed to answer the questions is contained in the rules, regulations, etc. which are cited.

2. **FOLLOWING DIRECTIONS (MAPS):** These questions test your ability to follow physical/geographic directions using street maps or building maps. You will have to read and understand a set of directions and then use them on a simple map.

3. **PREPARING WRITTEN MATERIAL:** These questions test for the ability to present information clearly and accurately, and to organize paragraphs logically and comprehensibly. For some questions, you will be given information in two or three sentences, followed by four restatements of the information. You must then choose the best version. For other questions, you will be given paragraphs with their sentences out of order. You must then choose, from among four choices, the best order for the sentences.

4. **PRINCIPLES AND PRACTICES OF SAFETY AND SECURITY:** These questions test for a knowledge of the proper principles and practices in the field of safety and security. The questions will cover such areas as selecting the best course of action to take in a safety or security related situation.

5. **SAFETY AND SECURITY METHODS AND PROCEDURES:** These questions test for knowledge of the methods and procedures utilized in safety and security related positions. The questions cover such areas as principles and practices of safety and security precautions in a building or grounds setting, accident prevention, proper response to safety or security related incidents, the investigation of incidents, and the inspection of buildings or grounds for potential safety and/or security problems.

INTRODUCTION – CONTINUED

6. **UNDERSTANDING AND INTERPRETING WRITTEN MATERIAL:** These questions test how well you comprehend written material. You will be provided with brief reading selections and will be asked questions about the selections. All the information required to answer the questions will be presented in the selections; you will not be required to have any special knowledge relating to the subject areas of the selections.

7. **SUPERVISION:** These questions test for knowledge of the principles and practices employed in planning, organizing, and controlling the activities of a work unit toward predetermined objectives. The concepts covered, usually in a situational question format, include such topics as assigning and reviewing work; evaluating performance; maintaining work standards; motivating and developing subordinates; implementing procedural change; increasing efficiency; and dealing with problems of absenteeism, morale, and discipline.

8. **ADMINISTRATIVE SUPERVISION:** These questions test for knowledge of the principles and practices involved in directing the activities of a large subordinate staff, including subordinate supervisors. Questions relate to the personal interactions between an upper level supervisor and his/her subordinate supervisors in the accomplishment of objectives. These questions cover such areas as assigning work to and coordinating the activities of several units, establishing and guiding staff development programs, evaluating the performance of subordinate supervisors, and maintaining relationships with other organizational sections.

The remainder of this test guide explains how you will be tested in each subject area listed above. A **TEST TASK** is provided for each subject area. This is an explanation of how a question is presented and how to correctly answer it. Read each explanation carefully. This test guide also provides at least one **SAMPLE QUESTION** for each subject area. The sample question is similar to the type of questions that will be presented on the actual test. This test guide provides the **SOLUTION** and correct answer to each sample question. You should study each sample question and solution in order to understand how the correct answer was determined.

At the end of this test guide we have included a **PRACTICE TEST** which includes additional examples of the types of questions you may see on your written test. Answers are provided in the Practice Test Key so that you can see how well you have done.

SUBJECT AREA 1

APPLYING WRITTEN INFORMATION IN A SAFETY AND SECURITY SETTING: These questions evaluate your ability to read, interpret and apply rules, regulations, directions, written narratives and other related material. You will be required to read a set of information and to appropriately apply the information to situations similar to those typically experienced in a public safety and security service setting. All information needed to answer the questions is contained in the rules, regulations, etc. which are cited.

TEST TASK: You will be given a set of rules, regulations, or other written information to read. You will then be asked a question which requires you to apply the rule to a given situation.

SAMPLE QUESTION:

RULE: While patrolling your grounds or building, keep a notebook and pencil with you. Keep the following emergency phone numbers in the notebook: police, fire department, nearby hospitals, alarm company, your supervisor, and the head of your building.

When you observe something out of the ordinary, take notes. Describe what is unusual, people who are unfamiliar, and any suspicious activity. If a crime or offense takes place, record what happened, who was involved, physical appearance of the suspect, clothing worn by the suspect, time and date, names and phone numbers of witnesses, where suspect was last seen, and any physical evidence found.

SITUATION: While you are doing your rounds at 11:20 p.m. you notice a door that has been left ajar. The door opens to the office of the Assistant Director of your facility. The door is typically closed and locked for the day when the Assistant Director leaves, usually between 5:00 and 6:00 p.m. The office is dark and no one is there.

QUESTION: Based solely on the above Rule and Situation, what, if anything, should be recorded in your notebook?

A. The office was dark when you entered it.
B. No one was in the office.
C. The door was open at 11:20 p.m.
D. No entry needs to be made.

The correct answer to this sample question is choice C.

SOLUTION: *The Situation states that while doing your rounds at 11:20 p.m., you notice a door left ajar. This door is typically closed and locked for the day between 5:00 and 6:00 p.m. by the Assistant Director. The question asks what, if anything, you should record about this incident in your notebook. To answer the question, evaluate all of the choices.*

Solution continued on next page.

SUBJECT AREA 1 – CONTINUED

Choice A states that you should record in your notebook the fact that the office was dark when you entered it. The Rule states that you should take notes when you observe something out of the ordinary. It is not out of the ordinary for the Assistant Director's office to be dark at 11:20 p.m. since the Assistant Director usually leaves for the day between 5:00 and 6:00 p.m. Choice A is incorrect.

Choice B states that you should record in your notebook the fact that no one was in the office. The Rule states that you should take notes when you observe something out of the ordinary. It is not out of the ordinary for the Assistant Director's office to be unoccupied at 11:20 p.m. since the Assistant Director is not usually at work after 6:00 p.m. Choice B is incorrect.

Choice C states that you should record in your notebook the fact that the door was open at 11:20 p.m. The Rule states that you should take notes when you observe something out of the ordinary. It is out of the ordinary for the Assistant Director's office door to be open at 11:20 p.m. because the door is typically closed and locked when the Assistant Director leaves for the day, usually between 5:00 and 6:00 p.m. Choice C is the correct answer.

Choice D states that you should make no entry in your notebook. The Rule states that you should take notes when you observe something out of the ordinary. It is out of the ordinary for the Assistant Director's office door to be open at 11:20 p.m. because the door is typically closed and locked when the Assistant Director leaves for the day, usually between 5:00 and 6:00 p.m. Choice D is incorrect.

SUBJECT AREA 2

FOLLOWING DIRECTIONS (MAPS): These questions test your ability to follow physical/geographic directions using street maps or building maps. You will have to read and understand a set of directions and then use them on a simple map.

TEST TASK: You will be provided with street maps or building maps. You will then be asked questions which require you to refer to the given maps and related information.

SAMPLE QUESTION:

DIRECTIONS: Base your answer to the following question on the sample information and sample map below. The map below shows a section of a city. The circled numbers are starting points and stopping points. Buildings are shown with letters. A roadblock is shown as a dark circle. One-way blocks are shown with an arrow pointing in the direction that you may travel on that block. For example:

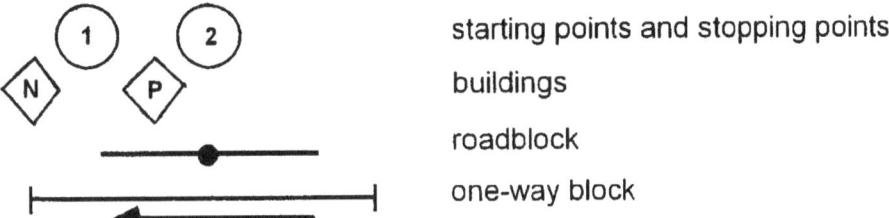

You may not go through a roadblock or travel in the wrong direction on a one-way block. You are to answer the question by finding and following the SHORTEST CORRECT route between the two locations given. All blocks are equal in length.

NOTE 1: Blocks may be traveled in either direction UNLESS only one direction is shown by an arrow for that block.

NOTE 2: You "pass" a building when you travel the block NEAREST the building.

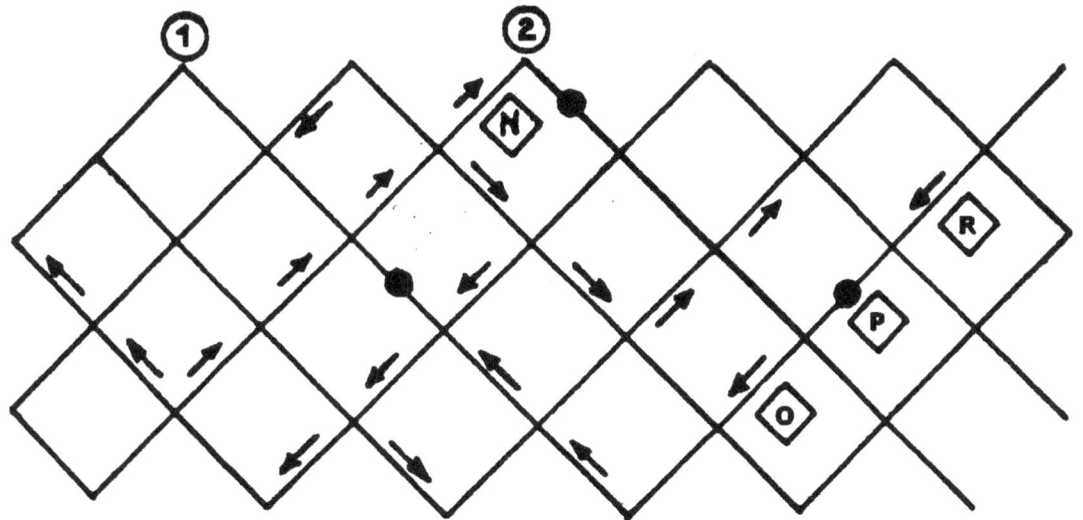

SUBJECT AREA 2 – CONTINUED

QUESTION: Which one of the following is a building you pass on the shortest correct route from point 1 to point 2?

A. N
B. O
C. P
D. R

The correct answer to this sample question is choice A.

SOLUTION:

Choice A *is the correct answer to this question. The shortest correct route from point 1 to point 2 is four blocks and passes only building N.*

Choice B *is not correct. You do not pass building O on the shortest correct route from point 1 to point 2.*

Choice C *is not correct. You do not pass building P on the shortest correct route from point 1 to point 2.*

Choice D *is not correct. You do not pass building R on the shortest correct route from point 1 to point 2.*

SUBJECT AREA 3

PREPARING WRITTEN MATERIAL: These questions test for the ability to present information clearly and accurately and for the ability to organize paragraphs logically and comprehensibly.

TEST TASK: There are two separate test tasks in this subject area.

- For the first, **Information Presentation**, you will be given information in two or three sentences, followed by four restatements of the information. You must then choose the best version.

- For the second, **Paragraph Organization**, you will be given paragraphs with their sentences out of order, and then be asked to choose, from among four choices, the best order for the sentences.

INFORMATION PRESENTATION SAMPLE QUESTION:

Martin Wilson failed to take proper precautions. His failure to take proper precautions caused a personal injury accident.

Which one of the following best presents the information above?

A. Martin Wilson failed to take proper precautions that caused a personal injury accident.
B. Proper precautions, which Martin Wilson failed to take, caused a personal injury accident.
C. Martin Wilson's failure to take proper precautions caused a personal injury accident.
D. Martin Wilson, who failed to take proper precautions, was in a personal injury accident.

The correct answer to this sample question is choice C.

SOLUTION:

Choice A *conveys the incorrect impression that proper precautions caused a personal injury accident.*

Choice B *conveys the incorrect impression that proper precautions caused a personal injury accident.*

Choice C *best presents the original information: Martin Wilson failed to take proper precautions and this failure caused a personal injury accident.*

Choice D *states that Martin Wilson was in a personal injury accident. The original information states that Martin Wilson caused a personal injury accident, but it does not state that Martin Wilson was in a personal injury accident.*

SUBJECT AREA 3 – CONTINUED

PARAGRAPH ORGANIZATION SAMPLE QUESTION:

The following question is based upon a group of sentences. The sentences are shown out of sequence, but when correctly arranged, they form a connected, well-organized paragraph. Read the sentences, and then answer the question about the best arrangement of these sentences.

1. Eventually, they piece all of this information together and make a choice.

2. Before actually deciding upon a human services job, people usually think about several possibilities.

3. They imagine themselves in different situations, and in so doing, they probably think about their interests, goals, and abilities.

4. Choosing among occupations in the field of human services is an important decision to make.

Which one of the following is the best arrangement of these sentences?

A. 2-4-1-3
B. 2-3-4-1
C. 4-2-1-3
D. 4-2-3-1

The correct answer to this sample question is choice D.

SOLUTION:

Choices A and C present the information in the paragraph out of logical sequence. In both A and C, sentence 1 comes before sentence 3. The key element in the organization of this paragraph is that sentence 3 contains the information to which sentence 1 refers; therefore, in logical sequence, sentence 3 should come before sentence 1.

Choice B also presents the information in the paragraph out of logical sequence. Choice B places the main idea of the paragraph (Sentence 4) in between two detail sentences (Sentences 1 and 3). The logical sequence of the information presented in the paragraph is therefore interrupted.

Choice D presents the information in the paragraph in the best logical sequence. Sentence 4 introduces the main idea of the paragraph: "choosing an occupation in the field of human services." Sentences 2-3-1 then follow up on this idea by describing, in order, the steps involved in making such a choice. Choice D is the best answer to this sample question.

SUBJECT AREA 4

PRINCIPLES AND PRACTICES OF SAFETY AND SECURITY: These questions test for a knowledge of the proper principles and practices in the field of safety and security. The questions will cover such areas as selecting the best course of action to take in a safety or security related situation.

TEST TASK: You will be presented with situations in which you must apply knowledge of the principles and practices of safety and security to answer the questions correctly.

SAMPLE QUESTION:

You are in charge of maintaining order in a room where a large number of people gather to transact business. A woman in the back of one of the lines starts to shout that she has been waiting for an hour and her line "has not moved at all." She continues to protest, and the rest of the crowd is getting restless.

Which one of the following actions would be best to take first in this situation?

A. Escort the woman to the head of the line and make sure her business is transacted promptly.
B. Tell the woman that unless she acts in a more orderly fashion, you will escort her out of the room.
C. Immediately remove the woman from the room.
D. Call the local police and detain the woman until the police arrive.

The correct answer to this sample question is choice B.

SOLUTION:

Choice A is not correct because escorting the woman to the head of the line and making sure her business is transacted promptly is not the best action to take first in this situation. This action could increase the restlessness of the other people who have also been waiting in the same line and will only serve to reinforce the woman's disruptive behavior.

Choice B is the correct answer because telling the woman that unless she acts in a more orderly fashion, you will escort her out of the room is the best action to take first in this situation. This action provides the woman with a clear warning to stop her disruptive behavior and advises her of the consequence should she continue to loudly protest the long wait.

Choice C is not correct because immediately removing the woman from the room is not the best action to take first in this situation. This action is too harsh based on the situation and could escalate the woman's disruptive behavior.

Choice D is not correct because calling the local police and detaining the woman until they arrive is not the best action to take first in this situation. This action is too harsh based on the situation and could escalate the woman's disruptive behavior.

SUBJECT AREA 5

SAFETY AND SECURITY METHODS AND PROCEDURES: These questions test for knowledge of the methods and procedures utilized in safety and security related positions. The questions cover such areas as principles and practices of safety and security precautions in a building or grounds setting, accident prevention, proper response to safety or security related incidents, the investigation of incidents, and the inspection of buildings or grounds for potential safety and/or security problems.

TEST TASK: You will be presented with questions in which you must apply knowledge of the methods and procedures utilized in safety and security related positions to answer the questions correctly.

SAMPLE QUESTION:

The most important purpose of patrolling the halls and grounds of a facility is to

A. discourage potential violations of rules or laws
B. give people on site the opportunity to obtain information or advice
C. maintain a routine observation of facility employees and their actions for your records
D. be able to provide assistance to local police authorities by accurately reporting whether unauthorized activity occurs in or near the facility

The correct answer to this sample question is choice A.

SOLUTION:

Choice A is the correct answer because discouraging potential violations of rules or laws is the most important purpose of patrolling the halls and grounds of a facility. Your presence while patrolling the halls and grounds of a facility may be enough to deter potential rule or law violators.

Choice B is not correct because giving people on site the opportunity to obtain information or advice is not the most important purpose of patrolling the halls and grounds of a facility. Although giving people on site the opportunity to obtain information or advice may be an important purpose of patrolling the halls and grounds of a facility, it is not the _most_ important purpose.

Choice C is not correct because maintaining a routine observation of facility employees and their actions for your records is not the most important purpose of patrolling the halls and grounds of a facility. Although maintaining a routine observation of facility employees and their actions for your records may be an important purpose of patrolling the halls and grounds of a facility, it is not the _most_ important purpose.

Choice D is not correct because being able to provide assistance to local police authorities by accurately reporting whether unauthorized activity occurs in or near the facility is not the most important purpose of patrolling the halls and grounds of a facility. Although being able to provide assistance to local police authorities by accurately reporting whether unauthorized activity occurs in or near the facility may be an important purpose of patrolling the halls and grounds of a facility, it is not the _most_ important purpose.

SUBJECT AREA 6

UNDERSTANDING AND INTERPRETING WRITTEN MATERIAL: These questions test how well you comprehend written material. You will be provided with brief reading selections and will be asked questions about the selections. All the information required to answer the questions will be presented in the selections; you will not be required to have any special knowledge relating to the subject areas of the selections.

TEST TASK: You will be provided with brief reading passages and then will be asked questions relating to the passages. All the information required to answer the questions will be provided in the passages.

SAMPLE QUESTION: "Increasingly, behavior termed 'road rage' is being viewed as a public health issue, because of the number of deaths and injuries related to it. Such behavior is often a reaction to the feeling that one has been treated unfairly by another driver, and it is much less likely to occur if a driver is treated fairly. 'Fair play' on the road includes the observance not only of traffic regulations but also of the rules of courtesy. Courteous driving is based on common sense consideration for other drivers and a strong desire to make the roads safe for everyone. Good highway manners should become just as much a matter of habit as other kinds of manners."

Which one of the following statements is best supported by the above selection?

A. Courteous driving contributes to road safety.
B. Those who are generally polite are also courteous drivers.
C. Unlike driving courtesy, the observance of traffic regulations is a matter of habit.
D. Being courteous when driving is more important than observing traffic regulations.

The correct answer to this sample question is choice A.

SOLUTION: To answer this question correctly, you must evaluate each choice against the written selection and determine the one that is best supported by the written selection.

Choice A *states, "Courteous driving contributes to road safety." Choice A is supported by the statement in the written selection that, "Courteous driving is based on...a strong desire to make the roads safe for everyone." This is the correct answer.*

Choice B *states, "Those who are generally polite are also courteous drivers." Choice B is not supported by the written selection. The written selection does not mention "those who are generally polite" at all. Choice B is not the correct answer to this question.*

Choice C *states, "Unlike driving courtesy, the observance of traffic regulations is a matter of habit." Choice C is not supported by the written selection. The written selection makes no such bold statement. Instead, the written material mildly suggests that "Good highway manners should become just as much a matter of habit as other kinds of manners." Choice C is not the correct answer to this question.*

Choice D *states, "Being courteous when driving is more important than observing traffic regulations." Choice D is not supported by the written selection. The written selection states, "'Fair play' on the road includes the observance not only of traffic regulations but also of the rules of courtesy." The written selection does not state that being courteous is more important than observing traffic regulations. Choice D is not the correct answer to this question.*

SUBJECT AREA 7

SUPERVISION: These questions test for knowledge of the principles and practices employed in planning, organizing, and controlling the activities of a work unit toward predetermined objectives. The concepts covered, usually in a situational question format, include such topics as assigning and reviewing work; evaluating performance; maintaining work standards; motivating and developing subordinates; implementing procedural change; increasing efficiency; and dealing with problems of absenteeism, morale, and discipline.

TEST TASK: You will be presented with situations in which you must apply knowledge of the principles and practices of supervision in order to answer the questions correctly.

SAMPLE QUESTION:
Assume that the unit you supervise is given a new work assignment and that you are unsure about the proper procedure to use in performing this assignment. Which one of the following actions should you take FIRST in this situation?

A. Obtain input from your staff.
B. Consult other unit supervisors who have had similar assignments.
C. Use an appropriate procedure from a similar assignment that you are familiar with.
D. Discuss the matter with your supervisor.

The correct answer to this sample question is choice D.

SOLUTION:

Choice A is not correct. Since this assignment is new for your unit, your staff would not be expected to be more knowledgeable than you about the proper procedure.

Choice B is not correct. Although discussing this matter with other supervisors may increase your knowledge of the new assignment, similar assignments performed in other units may differ in some important way from your new assignment. Other units may also function differently from your unit, so the procedures used to perform similar assignments may differ accordingly.

Choice C is not correct. Since this assignment is new for your unit, you would have no way of knowing whether the procedure from a similar assignment is appropriate to use. You would need someone with the appropriate knowledge, usually your supervisor, to determine if the procedure from a similar assignment could be used before you actually employed this procedure in the performance of your new assignment.

Choice D is the correct answer to this question. Your supervisor is more likely to be informed about what procedure may be appropriate for work that he or she assigns to you than would other unit supervisors or your staff. Even if your supervisor does not know what procedure is appropriate, a decision regarding which procedure to use should be made with his or her participation, since he or she has the ultimate responsibility for your unit's work.

SUBJECT AREA 8

ADMINISTRATIVE SUPERVISION: These questions test for knowledge of the principles and practices involved in directing the activities of a large subordinate staff, including subordinate supervisors. Questions relate to the personal interactions between an upper level supervisor and his/her subordinate supervisors in the accomplishment of objectives. These questions cover such areas as assigning work to and coordinating the activities of several units, establishing and guiding staff development programs, evaluating the performance of subordinate supervisors, and maintaining relationships with other organizational sections.

TEST TASK: You will be presented with situations in which you must apply knowledge of the principles and practices of administrative supervision to answer the questions correctly. You will be placed in the role of a supervisor of a section, which is made up of several units. Each unit has a supervisor and several employees. All unit supervisors report directly to you.

SAMPLE QUESTION:

You have delegated a work project to two unit supervisors and have asked them to collaborate on it. Later, you observe two employees strongly arguing about which one of them is responsible for a certain activity within the work project. The arguing employees work for different units. Which one of the following actions is most appropriate for you to take in this situation?

A. Intercede in the employees' argument and settle it.
B. Meet with the unit supervisors of the two employees and inform them of the situation you observed.
C. Inform one unit supervisor of the situation and ask this supervisor to take care of it.
D. Set up a meeting that includes both unit supervisors and both employees to resolve the situation.

The correct answer to this sample question is choice B.

SOLUTION:

Choice A *is not correct.* In your position, you supervise properly by giving direction through your unit supervisors. By taking this choice, you are not allowing your unit supervisors to handle a problem involving their staff members. Also, it is not reasonable that you would be able to settle the employees' dispute. Earlier, you delegated the work project to the two unit supervisors, who would be responsible for assigning activities related to the project. The two unit supervisors must deal with the problem.

Choice B *is the correct answer to this question.* The two unit supervisors are collaborating on the work project and therefore giving the assignments. You should meet with them and tell them about the employees' argument. The unit supervisors should be informed about the point of contention and the fact that the two employees had a heated argument. The unit supervisors must then work out a way to handle the situation.

Choice C *is not correct.* Speaking to only one supervisor about the situation means that the second supervisor may be uninformed, or only partly informed, about the situation. You cannot be assured that the first supervisor will include the second supervisor in finding a way to settle the issue. If the first unit supervisor chooses to handle the situation on his own and speak to both employees, this supervisor would be giving direction to one employee from another unit. This is not good supervisory practice. Also, in taking Choice C, you are favoring one supervisor and slighting the other.

Choice D *is not correct.* The unit supervisors need to come up with a way of handling the situation that you observed. To do this, they must be informed without the employees present. Also, by including the employees in the meeting, you may get a replay of their earlier argument, which is not helpful.

PRACTICE TEST

Below and on the following pages are additional examples of the types of questions that will be on the written test for the Safety and Security Series. The answers are given on page 25. Good luck!

APPLYING WRITTEN INFORMATION IN A SAFETY AND SECURITY SETTING

DIRECTIONS: The following two questions evaluate your ability to read and interpret a specific rule and apply it to a given situation or situations. Each question or set of questions is given with a **RULE** along with a **SITUATION** or situations. You should base your answers to these questions upon the information provided and **NOT** upon any other information you may have on the subject.

1. **RULE:** A security officer is to obey all lawful regulations of the employer and all orders of a police officer in police matters. The security officer is to assist and cooperate with police officers in preserving the peace. Where police are on the scene, on duty and off duty security personnel should identify themselves as security officers and offer assistance. The police officer's directives and judgment shall prevail.

SITUATION: When leaving work for the day, you see that a motor vehicle accident has taken place on the highway near your workplace. You approach the accident in your car and see that a police officer is on the scene. You inform the police officer that you are a security officer. Traffic is stopped.

According to the above Rule, under which one of the following conditions, if any, should you take control of directing traffic in this Situation?

A. The police officer instructs you to direct traffic.
B. You regularly direct traffic as part of your job.
C. You should not direct traffic because you are off duty.
D. You should not direct traffic because the highway is not on facility property.

2. **RULE:** If a law enforcement officer is required to be at a mental health facility, the officer will be required to lock his weapon in a designated gun cabinet and retain the only key. In areas where gun cabinets are not available, the law enforcement officer shall be asked to remove the bullets from his weapon and retain the weapon. The only other allowable option is for the officer to lock the weapon in his patrol car.

SITUATION: During rounds as a security officer in a mental health facility with no gun control cabinets available, you come upon a law enforcement officer whom you know to be a firearms instructor. You allow the officer to enter the building with his weapon.

Based solely on the above Rule and Situation, in which one of the following cases is your action correct?

A. The officer has stated that his police agency prohibits an officer from locking a weapon in his patrol car.
B. The officer has stated that he would be willing to put his weapon in a gun cabinet.
C. The officer has shown you a letter stating he must attend a meeting at the facility today on the topic of firearm instruction.
D. The officer has removed the bullets from his weapon.

FOLLOWING DIRECTIONS (MAPS)

DIRECTIONS: The following map presents a diagram of a floor of an office building. You should become familiar with the map and interpret it with the legend provided. Use the map to answer the questions on the next page.

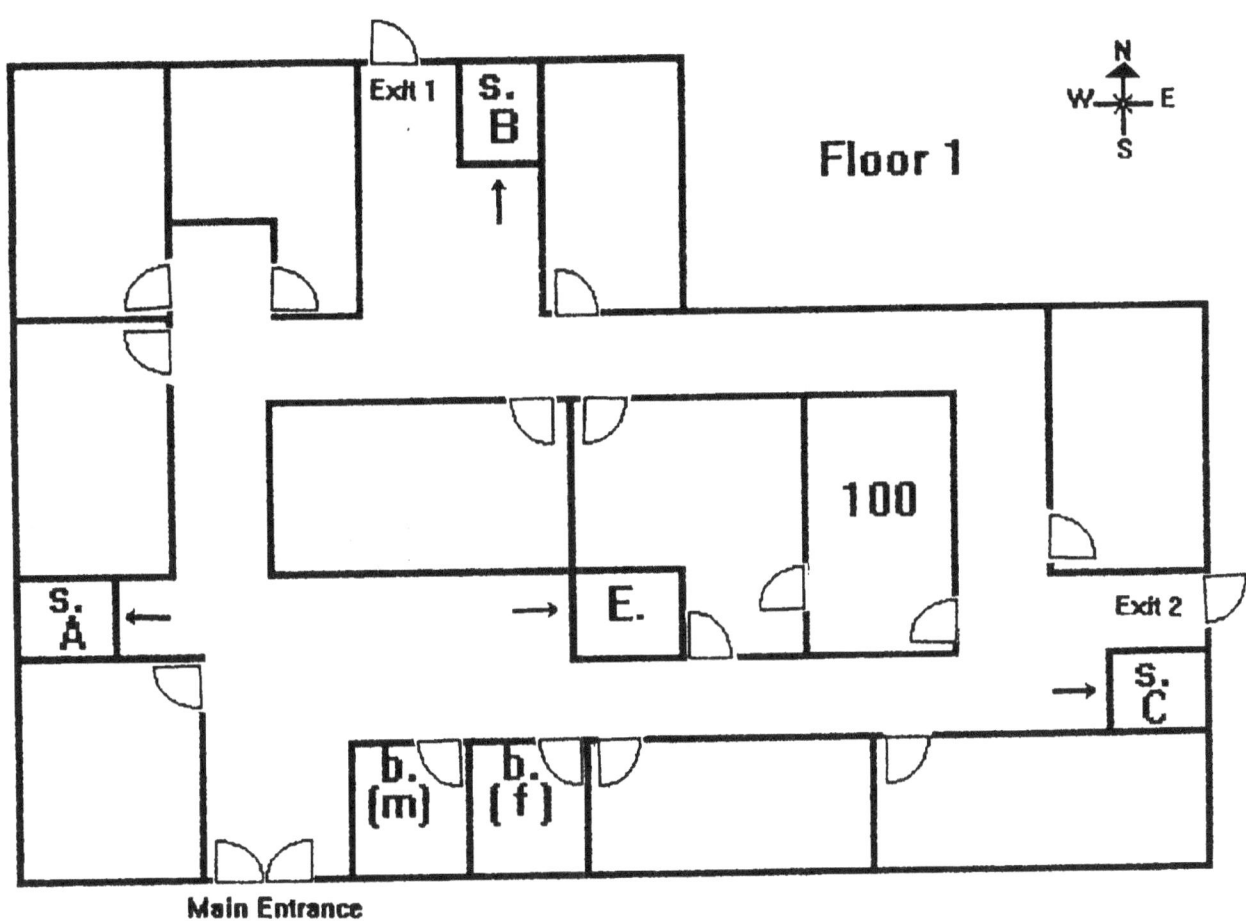

Legend:

Office Numbers appear inside the rooms; e.g., 100 = Office No. 100

E. = Elevator
s. = Stairwell; e.g., s.C = Stairwell C
b. = bathroom; e.g., b.(m) = bathroom (male)
              b.(f) = bathroom (female)

Assume that people receiving directions are able-bodied unless otherwise noted.

→ = the entrance to a stairwell or elevator used to access other floors in the building

◠ or ◡ = doors to an office or the building

FOLLOWING DIRECTIONS (MAPS) (Continued)

3. For a person in Office No. 100, which one of the following is the most direct route to leave the building in an emergency?

A. through exit 1
B. through exit 2
C. through stairwell C
D. through the Main Entrance

4. Which one of the following routes is the best to take if the elevator is out of service and a person standing directly inside the main entrance wants to get from Floor 1 to Floor 2 in the most efficient way?

A. Walk straight, take the second right, take the first left and take stairwell B to the second floor.
B. Walk straight, take the second right, walk straight, take the next right, take the first left and take stairwell C to the second floor.
C. Walk straight, take the first right, walk straight and take stairwell C to the second floor.
D. Walk straight, take the first left and take stairwell A to the second floor.

PREPARING WRITTEN MATERIAL

DIRECTIONS: Read the information given in the following two questions carefully. Then select the choice which presents the information most clearly, accurately, and completely.

5. Senator Martinez met with the county legislature. Then Senator Martinez announced that the meal subsidy program would start in June.

Which one of the following best presents the information given above?

A. After meeting with the county legislature, Senator Martinez announced that the meal subsidy program would start in June.
B. Senator Martinez met with the county legislature and announced that the meal subsidy program would start in June.
C. Senator Martinez announced that the meal subsidy program would start in June after a meeting with the county legislature.
D. Senator Martinez, who met with the county legislature, announced that the meal subsidy program would start in June.

6. Frank Colombe wrote the press release. He sent three copies to the Director. The Director then gave one of the copies to the Commissioner.

Which one of the following best presents the information given above?

A. Frank Colombe sent to the Director three copies of the press release he had written, who then gave a copy to the Commissioner.
B. Frank Colombe sent three copies of the press release he had written to the Director, who then gave one of the copies to the Commissioner.
C. The Director gave the Commissioner one of the three copies of the press release Frank Colombe had written and had been sent to him.
D. Of the three copies of the press release Frank Colombe had written and sent to the Director, one was then given to the Commissioner by him.

PREPARING WRITTEN MATERIAL (Continued)

DIRECTIONS: The following two (2) questions are based upon a group of sentences. The sentences are shown out of sequence, but when they are correctly arranged they form a connected, well-organized paragraph. Read the sentences and then answer the question about what order to arrange them in.

7.
1. The phosphates in detergents are carried into sewage systems, and from there into local rivers and streams, and eventually into large bodies of water.
2. The algae absorb much of the available oxygen that is necessary to sustain marine life.
3. There is no doubt that phosphates damage the environment through a complex chain of events.
4. Phosphates are nutrients, and, as such, they aid the growth of the algae living in the water.
5. This results not only in the death of fish and other aquatic life, but also in the too-thick growth of vegetation in the water.

Which one of the following is the best arrangement of these sentences?

A. 1-3-4-2-5
B. 1-4-2-5-3
C. 3-1-4-2-5
D. 3-4-2-1-5

8.
1. Never before has time been measured at a speed beyond the realm of experience.
2. Just how profound an effect it is having on society is as yet to be determined.
3. The computer has accelerated our sense of time beyond anything we have experienced before.
4. Though it is possible to conceive of an interval that brief and even to manipulate time at that speed, it is not possible to experience it.
5. It works in a time frame in which the nanosecond—a billionth of a second—is the primary measurement.

Which one of the following is the best arrangement of these sentences?

A. 1-2-3-5-4
B. 1-4-3-5-2
C. 3-2-5-4-1
D. 3-5-4-1-2

PRINCIPLES AND PRACTICES OF SAFETY AND SECURITY

9. You are on patrol in a radio-equipped car at night. You discover that a large drum of gasoline near a garage on the property is punctured and is rapidly spilling gasoline on the ground around the building.

Which one of the following actions should you take first in this situation?

A. Submit a written report of the incident to your supervisor.
B. Report the matter to headquarters.
C. Examine the puncture to see if it was accidental or deliberate.
D. Check other drums or containers around the building for punctures.

10. You hear shouting on the second floor of a building where you are on duty. Upon arriving at the scene, you see two building employees engaged in a fist fight in the hall.

Which one of the following actions should you take first in this situation?

A. Report the matter to the supervisors of the two employees.
B. Ask observers how the fight started.
C. Call for assistance.
D. Break up the fight.

SAFETY AND SECURITY METHODS AND PROCEDURES

11. Complaints relating to suspicious activity, especially at night, are often groundless. Which one of the following is the best way of handling such a complaint?

A. Analyze the nature of the complaint to make sure that it is justifiable before dispatching anyone to the scene.
B. Consider the complaint justified only if it corresponds to similar complaints in the same area.
C. Take no action on the complaint, but make a record of it.
D. Attend to the complaint immediately on the assumption that it is justified.

12. In the course of an investigation, you are interviewing a person who is over-talkative. Which one of the following is the best method for you to use in order to obtain the facts which you seek?

A. Tell the witness to talk only about the facts you are interested in.
B. Place a time limit on the witness's answers to your questions.
C. Make it clear that you want only "yes" or "no" answers to your questions.
D. Guide the conversation toward the subject of interest when the witness talks about subjects clearly not relevant to the interview.

UNDERSTANDING AND INTERPRETING WRITTEN MATERIAL

DIRECTIONS: The following two questions are related to the reading selection preceding each question. Base your answer to the question SOLELY on what is said in the selection – NOT on what you may happen to know about the subject discussed.

13. "The increasing demands upon our highways from a growing population and the development of forms of transportation not anticipated when the highways were first built have brought about congestion, confusion, and conflict, until the yearly toll of traffic accidents is now at an appalling level. If the death and disaster that traffic accidents bring throughout the year were concentrated into one calamity, we would shudder at the tremendous catastrophe. The loss is no less catastrophic because it is spread out over time and space."

Which one of the following statements concerning the yearly toll of traffic accidents is best supported by the passage above?

A. It is increasing the demands for safer means of transportation.
B. It has resulted in increased congestion, confusion, and conflict on our highways.
C. It has resulted mainly from the new forms of transportation.
D. It does not shock us as much as it should because the accidents do not all occur at the same time.

14. "Depression is one of the top public health problems in the United States, and its occurrence is on the rise. One in 20 Americans develops a case of depression serious enough to require professional treatment. The incidence of depression has been escalating among Baby Boomers (Americans born in the years 1946 through 1964). The reason for this increase is that the lifestyles of this generation have become increasingly demanding while offering little support. Also, stress and poor eating habits are now more the rule than the exception, and both can disrupt brain chemistry enough to bring on depression."

Which one of the following statements is best supported by the above selection?

A. We can expect a small proportion of the population to require treatment for depression at some time in their lives.
B. Baby Boomers have the highest rate of depression in the United States.
C. Lifestyle demands are the major cause of depression in the current generation.
D. Depression can cause a disruption in the chemistry of the brain.

SUPERVISION

DIRECTIONS: For the following two questions, assume that you are the newly appointed supervisor of a unit consisting of several employees. You report to a section head.

15. You have a suspicion that some of your employees are not working to the best of their abilities. Which one of the following actions should you take first in this situation?

A. Arrange for these employees to take a course in organizing priorities.
B. Determine which employee is the worst offender.
C. Assess the assignments and work methods of these employees.
D. Set up a meeting with these employees to learn about any work problems they are having.

16. As you are giving an employee a certain assignment, she expresses concern that it is too difficult. The employee is reluctant to accept the assignment. Which one of the following actions should you take first in this situation?

A. Insist that the employee take on the assignment.
B. Tell the employee that it is likely she has completed assignments of similar difficulty before.
C. Offer to share the tasks of the assignment with the employee.
D. Ask the employee why she sees the assignment as difficult.

ADMINISTRATIVE SUPERVISION

DIRECTIONS: For the following two questions, assume that you supervise a section composed of several units. Each unit has a supervisor and several employees. All unit supervisors report directly to you.

17. Assume that you are the head of a section made up of four units, each of which is responsible for similar work. The work volume of one of the units of the section has permanently decreased to the point that the supervisor of that unit now is responsible for much less work than any of the other three unit supervisors. Of the following, which determination should you as the section head make first in this situation?

A. Can other or additional tasks be assigned to this unit?
B. Can the unit supervisor function as assistant section head?
C. Can the unit supervisor's position be reclassified or reallocated?
D. Can the section be reorganized into three units?

18. In which one of the following circumstances should you try to reduce turnover in the section you supervise?

A. The turnover is higher than that of other sections.
B. The turnover reduces the number of highly experienced employees.
C. The turnover lowers the efficiency of the section.
D. The turnover requires unit supervisors to spend a moderate amount of time in training new employees.

PRACTICE TEST KEY

(1) A
(2) D
(3) B
(4) D
(5) A
(6) B
(7) C
(8) D
(9) B
(10) C
(11) D
(12) D
(13) D
(14) A
(15) C
(16) D
(17) A
(18) C

HOW TO TAKE A TEST

I. YOU MUST PASS AN EXAMINATION

A. *WHAT EVERY CANDIDATE SHOULD KNOW*

Examination applicants often ask us for help in preparing for the written test. What can I study in advance? What kinds of questions will be asked? How will the test be given? How will the papers be graded?

As an applicant for a civil service examination, you may be wondering about some of these things. Our purpose here is to suggest effective methods of advance study and to describe civil service examinations.

Your chances for success on this examination can be increased if you know how to prepare. Those "pre-examination jitters" can be reduced if you know what to expect. You can even experience an adventure in good citizenship if you know why civil service exams are given.

B. *WHY ARE CIVIL SERVICE EXAMINATIONS GIVEN?*

Civil service examinations are important to you in two ways. As a citizen, you want public jobs filled by employees who know how to do their work. As a job seeker, you want a fair chance to compete for that job on an equal footing with other candidates. The best-known means of accomplishing this two-fold goal is the competitive examination.

Exams are widely publicized throughout the nation. They may be administered for jobs in federal, state, city, municipal, town or village governments or agencies.

Any citizen may apply, with some limitations, such as the age or residence of applicants. Your experience and education may be reviewed to see whether you meet the requirements for the particular examination. When these requirements exist, they are reasonable and applied consistently to all applicants. Thus, a competitive examination may cause you some uneasiness now, but it is your privilege and safeguard.

C. *HOW ARE CIVIL SERVICE EXAMS DEVELOPED?*

Examinations are carefully written by trained technicians who are specialists in the field known as "psychological measurement," in consultation with recognized authorities in the field of work that the test will cover. These experts recommend the subject matter areas or skills to be tested; only those knowledges or skills important to your success on the job are included. The most reliable books and source materials available are used as references. Together, the experts and technicians judge the difficulty level of the questions.

Test technicians know how to phrase questions so that the problem is clearly stated. Their ethics do not permit "trick" or "catch" questions. Questions may have been tried out on sample groups, or subjected to statistical analysis, to determine their usefulness.

Written tests are often used in combination with performance tests, ratings of training and experience, and oral interviews. All of these measures combine to form the best-known means of finding the right person for the right job.

II. HOW TO PASS THE WRITTEN TEST

A. NATURE OF THE EXAMINATION

To prepare intelligently for civil service examinations, you should know how they differ from school examinations you have taken. In school you were assigned certain definite pages to read or subjects to cover. The examination questions were quite detailed and usually emphasized memory. Civil service exams, on the other hand, try to discover your present ability to perform the duties of a position, plus your potentiality to learn these duties. In other words, a civil service exam attempts to predict how successful you will be. Questions cover such a broad area that they cannot be as minute and detailed as school exam questions.

In the public service similar kinds of work, or positions, are grouped together in one "class." This process is known as *position-classification*. All the positions in a class are paid according to the salary range for that class. One class title covers all of these positions, and they are all tested by the same examination.

B. FOUR BASIC STEPS

1) Study the announcement

How, then, can you know what subjects to study? Our best answer is: "Learn as much as possible about the class of positions for which you've applied." The exam will test the knowledge, skills and abilities needed to do the work.

Your most valuable source of information about the position you want is the official exam announcement. This announcement lists the training and experience qualifications. Check these standards and apply only if you come reasonably close to meeting them.

The brief description of the position in the examination announcement offers some clues to the subjects which will be tested. Think about the job itself. Review the duties in your mind. Can you perform them, or are there some in which you are rusty? Fill in the blank spots in your preparation.

Many jurisdictions preview the written test in the exam announcement by including a section called "Knowledge and Abilities Required," "Scope of the Examination," or some similar heading. Here you will find out specifically what fields will be tested.

2) Review your own background

Once you learn in general what the position is all about, and what you need to know to do the work, ask yourself which subjects you already know fairly well and which need improvement. You may wonder whether to concentrate on improving your strong areas or on building some background in your fields of weakness. When the announcement has specified "some knowledge" or "considerable knowledge," or has used adjectives like "beginning principles of…" or "advanced … methods," you can get a clue as to the number and difficulty of questions to be asked in any given field. More questions, and hence broader coverage, would be included for those subjects which are more important in the work. Now weigh your strengths and weaknesses against the job requirements and prepare accordingly.

3) Determine the level of the position

Another way to tell how intensively you should prepare is to understand the level of the job for which you are applying. Is it the entering level? In other words, is this the position in which beginners in a field of work are hired? Or is it an intermediate or advanced level? Sometimes this is indicated by such words as "Junior" or "Senior" in the class title. Other jurisdictions use Roman numerals to designate the level – Clerk I, Clerk II, for example. The word "Supervisor" sometimes appears in the title. If the level is not indicated by the title, check the description of duties. Will you be working under very close supervision, or will you have responsibility for independent decisions in this work?

4) Choose appropriate study materials

Now that you know the subjects to be examined and the relative amount of each subject to be covered, you can choose suitable study materials. For beginning level jobs, or even advanced ones, if you have a pronounced weakness in some aspect of your training, read a modern, standard textbook in that field. Be sure it is up to date and has general coverage. Such books are normally available at your library, and the librarian will be glad to help you locate one. For entry-level positions, questions of appropriate difficulty are chosen – neither highly advanced questions, nor those too simple. Such questions require careful thought but not advanced training.

If the position for which you are applying is technical or advanced, you will read more advanced, specialized material. If you are already familiar with the basic principles of your field, elementary textbooks would waste your time. Concentrate on advanced textbooks and technical periodicals. Think through the concepts and review difficult problems in your field.

These are all general sources. You can get more ideas on your own initiative, following these leads. For example, training manuals and publications of the government agency which employs workers in your field can be useful, particularly for technical and professional positions. A letter or visit to the government department involved may result in more specific study suggestions, and certainly will provide you with a more definite idea of the exact nature of the position you are seeking.

III. KINDS OF TESTS

Tests are used for purposes other than measuring knowledge and ability to perform specified duties. For some positions, it is equally important to test ability to make adjustments to new situations or to profit from training. In others, basic mental abilities not dependent on information are essential. Questions which test these things may not appear as pertinent to the duties of the position as those which test for knowledge and information. Yet they are often highly important parts of a fair examination. For very general questions, it is almost impossible to help you direct your study efforts. What we can do is to point out some of the more common of these general abilities needed in public service positions and describe some typical questions.

1) General information

Broad, general information has been found useful for predicting job success in some kinds of work. This is tested in a variety of ways, from vocabulary lists to questions about current events. Basic background in some field of work, such as sociology or economics, may be sampled in a group of questions. Often these are principles which have become familiar to most persons through exposure rather than through formal training. It is difficult to advise you how to study for these questions; being alert to the world around you is our best suggestion.

2) Verbal ability

An example of an ability needed in many positions is verbal or language ability. Verbal ability is, in brief, the ability to use and understand words. Vocabulary and grammar tests are typical measures of this ability. Reading comprehension or paragraph interpretation questions are common in many kinds of civil service tests. You are given a paragraph of written material and asked to find its central meaning.

3) Numerical ability

Number skills can be tested by the familiar arithmetic problem, by checking paired lists of numbers to see which are alike and which are different, or by interpreting charts and graphs. In the latter test, a graph may be printed in the test booklet which you are asked to use as the basis for answering questions.

4) Observation

A popular test for law-enforcement positions is the observation test. A picture is shown to you for several minutes, then taken away. Questions about the picture test your ability to observe both details and larger elements.

5) Following directions

In many positions in the public service, the employee must be able to carry out written instructions dependably and accurately. You may be given a chart with several columns, each column listing a variety of information. The questions require you to carry out directions involving the information given in the chart.

6) Skills and aptitudes

Performance tests effectively measure some manual skills and aptitudes. When the skill is one in which you are trained, such as typing or shorthand, you can practice. These tests are often very much like those given in business school or high school courses. For many of the other skills and aptitudes, however, no short-time preparation can be made. Skills and abilities natural to you or that you have developed throughout your lifetime are being tested.

Many of the general questions just described provide all the data needed to answer the questions and ask you to use your reasoning ability to find the answers. Your best preparation for these tests, as well as for tests of facts and ideas, is to be at your physical and mental best. You, no doubt, have your own methods of getting into an exam-taking mood and keeping "in shape." The next section lists some ideas on this subject.

IV. KINDS OF QUESTIONS

Only rarely is the "essay" question, which you answer in narrative form, used in civil service tests. Civil service tests are usually of the short-answer type. Full instructions for answering these questions will be given to you at the examination. But in case this is your first experience with short-answer questions and separate answer sheets, here is what you need to know:

1) Multiple-choice Questions

Most popular of the short-answer questions is the "multiple choice" or "best answer" question. It can be used, for example, to test for factual knowledge, ability to solve problems or judgment in meeting situations found at work.

A multiple-choice question is normally one of three types—

- It can begin with an incomplete statement followed by several possible endings. You are to find the one ending which *best* completes the statement, although some of the others may not be entirely wrong.
- It can also be a complete statement in the form of a question which is answered by choosing one of the statements listed.

- It can be in the form of a problem – again you select the best answer.

Here is an example of a multiple-choice question with a discussion which should give you some clues as to the method for choosing the right answer:

When an employee has a complaint about his assignment, the action which will *best* help him overcome his difficulty is to
- A. discuss his difficulty with his coworkers
- B. take the problem to the head of the organization
- C. take the problem to the person who gave him the assignment
- D. say nothing to anyone about his complaint

In answering this question, you should study each of the choices to find which is best. Consider choice "A" – Certainly an employee may discuss his complaint with fellow employees, but no change or improvement can result, and the complaint remains unresolved. Choice "B" is a poor choice since the head of the organization probably does not know what assignment you have been given, and taking your problem to him is known as "going over the head" of the supervisor. The supervisor, or person who made the assignment, is the person who can clarify it or correct any injustice. Choice "C" is, therefore, correct. To say nothing, as in choice "D," is unwise. Supervisors have and interest in knowing the problems employees are facing, and the employee is seeking a solution to his problem.

2) True/False Questions

The "true/false" or "right/wrong" form of question is sometimes used. Here a complete statement is given. Your job is to decide whether the statement is right or wrong.

SAMPLE: A roaming cell-phone call to a nearby city costs less than a non-roaming call to a distant city.

This statement is wrong, or false, since roaming calls are more expensive.

This is not a complete list of all possible question forms, although most of the others are variations of these common types. You will always get complete directions for answering questions. Be sure you understand *how* to mark your answers – ask questions until you do.

V. RECORDING YOUR ANSWERS

Computer terminals are used more and more today for many different kinds of exams.

For an examination with very few applicants, you may be told to record your answers in the test booklet itself. Separate answer sheets are much more common. If this separate answer sheet is to be scored by machine – and this is often the case – it is highly important that you mark your answers correctly in order to get credit.

An electronic scoring machine is often used in civil service offices because of the speed with which papers can be scored. Machine-scored answer sheets must be marked with a pencil, which will be given to you. This pencil has a high graphite content which responds to the electronic scoring machine. As a matter of fact, stray dots may register as answers, so do not let your pencil rest on the answer sheet while you are pondering the correct answer. Also, if your pencil lead breaks or is otherwise defective, ask for another.

Since the answer sheet will be dropped in a slot in the scoring machine, be careful not to bend the corners or get the paper crumpled.

The answer sheet normally has five vertical columns of numbers, with 30 numbers to a column. These numbers correspond to the question numbers in your test booklet. After each number, going across the page are four or five pairs of dotted lines. These short dotted lines have small letters or numbers above them. The first two pairs may also have a "T" or "F" above the letters. This indicates that the first two pairs only are to be used if the questions are of the true-false type. If the questions are multiple choice, disregard the "T" and "F" and pay attention only to the small letters or numbers.

Answer your questions in the manner of the sample that follows:

32. The largest city in the United States is
    A. Washington, D.C.
    B. New York City
    C. Chicago
    D. Detroit
    E. San Francisco

1) Choose the answer you think is best. (New York City is the largest, so "B" is correct.)
2) Find the row of dotted lines numbered the same as the question you are answering. (Find row number 32)
3) Find the pair of dotted lines corresponding to the answer. (Find the pair of lines under the mark "B.")
4) Make a solid black mark between the dotted lines.

VI. BEFORE THE TEST

Common sense will help you find procedures to follow to get ready for an examination. Too many of us, however, overlook these sensible measures. Indeed, nervousness and fatigue have been found to be the most serious reasons why applicants fail to do their best on civil service tests. Here is a list of reminders:

- Begin your preparation early – Don't wait until the last minute to go scurrying around for books and materials or to find out what the position is all about.
- Prepare continuously – An hour a night for a week is better than an all-night cram session. This has been definitely established. What is more, a night a week for a month will return better dividends than crowding your study into a shorter period of time.
- Locate the place of the exam – You have been sent a notice telling you when and where to report for the examination. If the location is in a different town or otherwise unfamiliar to you, it would be well to inquire the best route and learn something about the building.
- Relax the night before the test – Allow your mind to rest. Do not study at all that night. Plan some mild recreation or diversion; then go to bed early and get a good night's sleep.
- Get up early enough to make a leisurely trip to the place for the test – This way unforeseen events, traffic snarls, unfamiliar buildings, etc. will not upset you.
- Dress comfortably – A written test is not a fashion show. You will be known by number and not by name, so wear something comfortable.

- Leave excess paraphernalia at home – Shopping bags and odd bundles will get in your way. You need bring only the items mentioned in the official notice you received; usually everything you need is provided. Do not bring reference books to the exam. They will only confuse those last minutes and be taken away from you when in the test room.
- Arrive somewhat ahead of time – If because of transportation schedules you must get there very early, bring a newspaper or magazine to take your mind off yourself while waiting.
- Locate the examination room – When you have found the proper room, you will be directed to the seat or part of the room where you will sit. Sometimes you are given a sheet of instructions to read while you are waiting. Do not fill out any forms until you are told to do so; just read them and be prepared.
- Relax and prepare to listen to the instructions
- If you have any physical problem that may keep you from doing your best, be sure to tell the test administrator. If you are sick or in poor health, you really cannot do your best on the exam. You can come back and take the test some other time.

VII. AT THE TEST

The day of the test is here and you have the test booklet in your hand. The temptation to get going is very strong. Caution! There is more to success than knowing the right answers. You must know how to identify your papers and understand variations in the type of short-answer question used in this particular examination. Follow these suggestions for maximum results from your efforts:

1) Cooperate with the monitor

The test administrator has a duty to create a situation in which you can be as much at ease as possible. He will give instructions, tell you when to begin, check to see that you are marking your answer sheet correctly, and so on. He is not there to guard you, although he will see that your competitors do not take unfair advantage. He wants to help you do your best.

2) Listen to all instructions

Don't jump the gun! Wait until you understand all directions. In most civil service tests you get more time than you need to answer the questions. So don't be in a hurry. Read each word of instructions until you clearly understand the meaning. Study the examples, listen to all announcements and follow directions. Ask questions if you do not understand what to do.

3) Identify your papers

Civil service exams are usually identified by number only. You will be assigned a number; you must not put your name on your test papers. Be sure to copy your number correctly. Since more than one exam may be given, copy your exact examination title.

4) Plan your time

Unless you are told that a test is a "speed" or "rate of work" test, speed itself is usually not important. Time enough to answer all the questions will be provided, but this does not mean that you have all day. An overall time limit has been set. Divide the total time (in minutes) by the number of questions to determine the approximate time you have for each question.

5) Do not linger over difficult questions

If you come across a difficult question, mark it with a paper clip (useful to have along) and come back to it when you have been through the booklet. One caution if you do this – be sure to skip a number on your answer sheet as well. Check often to be sure that you have not lost your place and that you are marking in the row numbered the same as the question you are answering.

6) Read the questions

Be sure you know what the question asks! Many capable people are unsuccessful because they failed to *read* the questions correctly.

7) Answer all questions

Unless you have been instructed that a penalty will be deducted for incorrect answers, it is better to guess than to omit a question.

8) Speed tests

It is often better NOT to guess on speed tests. It has been found that on timed tests people are tempted to spend the last few seconds before time is called in marking answers at random – without even reading them – in the hope of picking up a few extra points. To discourage this practice, the instructions may warn you that your score will be "corrected" for guessing. That is, a penalty will be applied. The incorrect answers will be deducted from the correct ones, or some other penalty formula will be used.

9) Review your answers

If you finish before time is called, go back to the questions you guessed or omitted to give them further thought. Review other answers if you have time.

10) Return your test materials

If you are ready to leave before others have finished or time is called, take ALL your materials to the monitor and leave quietly. Never take any test material with you. The monitor can discover whose papers are not complete, and taking a test booklet may be grounds for disqualification.

VIII. EXAMINATION TECHNIQUES

1) Read the general instructions carefully. These are usually printed on the first page of the exam booklet. As a rule, these instructions refer to the timing of the examination; the fact that you should not start work until the signal and must stop work at a signal, etc. If there are any *special* instructions, such as a choice of questions to be answered, make sure that you note this instruction carefully.

2) When you are ready to start work on the examination, that is as soon as the signal has been given, read the instructions to each question booklet, underline any key words or phrases, such as *least, best, outline, describe* and the like. In this way you will tend to answer as requested rather than discover on reviewing your paper that you *listed without describing*, that you selected the *worst* choice rather than the *best* choice, etc.

3) If the examination is of the objective or multiple-choice type – that is, each question will also give a series of possible answers: A, B, C or D, and you are called upon to select the best answer and write the letter next to that answer on your answer paper – it is advisable to start answering each question in turn. There may be anywhere from 50 to 100 such questions in the three or four hours allotted and you can see how much time would be taken if you read through all the questions before beginning to answer any. Furthermore, if you come across a question or group of questions which you know would be difficult to answer, it would undoubtedly affect your handling of all the other questions.

4) If the examination is of the essay type and contains but a few questions, it is a moot point as to whether you should read all the questions before starting to answer any one. Of course, if you are given a choice – say five out of seven and the like – then it is essential to read all the questions so you can eliminate the two that are most difficult. If, however, you are asked to answer all the questions, there may be danger in trying to answer the easiest one first because you may find that you will spend too much time on it. The best technique is to answer the first question, then proceed to the second, etc.

5) Time your answers. Before the exam begins, write down the time it started, then add the time allowed for the examination and write down the time it must be completed, then divide the time available somewhat as follows:
   - If 3-1/2 hours are allowed, that would be 210 minutes. If you have 80 objective-type questions, that would be an average of 2-1/2 minutes per question. Allow yourself no more than 2 minutes per question, or a total of 160 minutes, which will permit about 50 minutes to review.
   - If for the time allotment of 210 minutes there are 7 essay questions to answer, that would average about 30 minutes a question. Give yourself only 25 minutes per question so that you have about 35 minutes to review.

6) The most important instruction is to *read each question* and make sure you know what is wanted. The second most important instruction is to *time yourself properly* so that you answer every question. The third most important instruction is to *answer every question*. Guess if you have to but include something for each question. Remember that you will receive no credit for a blank and will probably receive some credit if you write something in answer to an essay question. If you guess a letter – say "B" for a multiple-choice question – you may have guessed right. If you leave a blank as an answer to a multiple-choice question, the examiners may respect your feelings but it will not add a point to your score. Some exams may penalize you for wrong answers, so in such cases *only*, you may not want to guess unless you have some basis for your answer.

7) Suggestions
   a. Objective-type questions
      1. Examine the question booklet for proper sequence of pages and questions
      2. Read all instructions carefully
      3. Skip any question which seems too difficult; return to it after all other questions have been answered
      4. Apportion your time properly; do not spend too much time on any single question or group of questions

5. Note and underline key words – *all, most, fewest, least, best, worst, same, opposite,* etc.
6. Pay particular attention to negatives
7. Note unusual option, e.g., unduly long, short, complex, different or similar in content to the body of the question
8. Observe the use of "hedging" words – *probably, may, most likely,* etc.
9. Make sure that your answer is put next to the same number as the question
10. Do not second-guess unless you have good reason to believe the second answer is definitely more correct
11. Cross out original answer if you decide another answer is more accurate; do not erase until you are ready to hand your paper in
12. Answer all questions; guess unless instructed otherwise
13. Leave time for review

   b. Essay questions
     1. Read each question carefully
     2. Determine exactly what is wanted. Underline key words or phrases.
     3. Decide on outline or paragraph answer
     4. Include many different points and elements unless asked to develop any one or two points or elements
     5. Show impartiality by giving pros and cons unless directed to select one side only
     6. Make and write down any assumptions you find necessary to answer the questions
     7. Watch your English, grammar, punctuation and choice of words
     8. Time your answers; don't crowd material

8) Answering the essay question

Most essay questions can be answered by framing the specific response around several key words or ideas. Here are a few such key words or ideas:

M's: manpower, materials, methods, money, management
P's: purpose, program, policy, plan, procedure, practice, problems, pitfalls, personnel, public relations

   a. Six basic steps in handling problems:
     1. Preliminary plan and background development
     2. Collect information, data and facts
     3. Analyze and interpret information, data and facts
     4. Analyze and develop solutions as well as make recommendations
     5. Prepare report and sell recommendations
     6. Install recommendations and follow up effectiveness

   b. Pitfalls to avoid
     1. *Taking things for granted* – A statement of the situation does not necessarily imply that each of the elements is necessarily true; for example, a complaint may be invalid and biased so that all that can be taken for granted is that a complaint has been registered

2. *Considering only one side of a situation* – Wherever possible, indicate several alternatives and then point out the reasons you selected the best one
3. *Failing to indicate follow up* – Whenever your answer indicates action on your part, make certain that you will take proper follow-up action to see how successful your recommendations, procedures or actions turn out to be
4. *Taking too long in answering any single question* – Remember to time your answers properly

IX. AFTER THE TEST

Scoring procedures differ in detail among civil service jurisdictions although the general principles are the same. Whether the papers are hand-scored or graded by machine we have described, they are nearly always graded by number. That is, the person who marks the paper knows only the number – never the name – of the applicant. Not until all the papers have been graded will they be matched with names. If other tests, such as training and experience or oral interview ratings have been given, scores will be combined. Different parts of the examination usually have different weights. For example, the written test might count 60 percent of the final grade, and a rating of training and experience 40 percent. In many jurisdictions, veterans will have a certain number of points added to their grades.

After the final grade has been determined, the names are placed in grade order and an eligible list is established. There are various methods for resolving ties between those who get the same final grade – probably the most common is to place first the name of the person whose application was received first. Job offers are made from the eligible list in the order the names appear on it. You will be notified of your grade and your rank as soon as all these computations have been made. This will be done as rapidly as possible.

People who are found to meet the requirements in the announcement are called "eligibles." Their names are put on a list of eligible candidates. An eligible's chances of getting a job depend on how high he stands on this list and how fast agencies are filling jobs from the list.

When a job is to be filled from a list of eligibles, the agency asks for the names of people on the list of eligibles for that job. When the civil service commission receives this request, it sends to the agency the names of the three people highest on this list. Or, if the job to be filled has specialized requirements, the office sends the agency the names of the top three persons who meet these requirements from the general list.

The appointing officer makes a choice from among the three people whose names were sent to him. If the selected person accepts the appointment, the names of the others are put back on the list to be considered for future openings.

That is the rule in hiring from all kinds of eligible lists, whether they are for typist, carpenter, chemist, or something else. For every vacancy, the appointing officer has his choice of any one of the top three eligibles on the list. This explains why the person whose name is on top of the list sometimes does not get an appointment when some of the persons lower on the list do. If the appointing officer chooses the second or third eligible, the No. 1 eligible does not get a job at once, but stays on the list until he is appointed or the list is terminated.

X. HOW TO PASS THE INTERVIEW TEST

The examination for which you applied requires an oral interview test. You have already taken the written test and you are now being called for the interview test – the final part of the formal examination.

You may think that it is not possible to prepare for an interview test and that there are no procedures to follow during an interview. Our purpose is to point out some things you can do in advance that will help you and some good rules to follow and pitfalls to avoid while you are being interviewed.

What is an interview supposed to test?

The written examination is designed to test the technical knowledge and competence of the candidate; the oral is designed to evaluate intangible qualities, not readily measured otherwise, and to establish a list showing the relative fitness of each candidate – as measured against his competitors – for the position sought. Scoring is not on the basis of "right" and "wrong," but on a sliding scale of values ranging from "not passable" to "outstanding." As a matter of fact, it is possible to achieve a relatively low score without a single "incorrect" answer because of evident weakness in the qualities being measured.

Occasionally, an examination may consist entirely of an oral test – either an individual or a group oral. In such cases, information is sought concerning the technical knowledges and abilities of the candidate, since there has been no written examination for this purpose. More commonly, however, an oral test is used to supplement a written examination.

Who conducts interviews?

The composition of oral boards varies among different jurisdictions. In nearly all, a representative of the personnel department serves as chairman. One of the members of the board may be a representative of the department in which the candidate would work. In some cases, "outside experts" are used, and, frequently, a businessman or some other representative of the general public is asked to serve. Labor and management or other special groups may be represented. The aim is to secure the services of experts in the appropriate field.

However the board is composed, it is a good idea (and not at all improper or unethical) to ascertain in advance of the interview who the members are and what groups they represent. When you are introduced to them, you will have some idea of their backgrounds and interests, and at least you will not stutter and stammer over their names.

What should be done before the interview?

While knowledge about the board members is useful and takes some of the surprise element out of the interview, there is other preparation which is more substantive. It *is* possible to prepare for an oral interview – in several ways:

1) Keep a copy of your application and review it carefully before the interview

This may be the only document before the oral board, and the starting point of the interview. Know what education and experience you have listed there, and the sequence and dates of all of it. Sometimes the board will ask you to review the highlights of your experience for them; you should not have to hem and haw doing it.

2) Study the class specification and the examination announcement

Usually, the oral board has one or both of these to guide them. The qualities, characteristics or knowledges required by the position sought are stated in these documents. They offer valuable clues as to the nature of the oral interview. For example, if the job involves supervisory responsibilities, the announcement will usually indicate that knowledge of modern supervisory methods and the qualifications of the candidate as a supervisor will be tested. If so, you can expect such questions, frequently in the form of a hypothetical situation which you are expected to solve. NEVER go into an oral without knowledge of the duties and responsibilities of the job you seek.

3) Think through each qualification required

Try to visualize the kind of questions you would ask if you were a board member. How well could you answer them? Try especially to appraise your own knowledge and background in each area, *measured against the job sought*, and identify any areas in which you are weak. Be critical and realistic – do not flatter yourself.

4) Do some general reading in areas in which you feel you may be weak

For example, if the job involves supervision and your past experience has NOT, some general reading in supervisory methods and practices, particularly in the field of human relations, might be useful. Do NOT study agency procedures or detailed manuals. The oral board will be testing your understanding and capacity, not your memory.

5) Get a good night's sleep and watch your general health and mental attitude

You will want a clear head at the interview. Take care of a cold or any other minor ailment, and of course, no hangovers.

What should be done on the day of the interview?

Now comes the day of the interview itself. Give yourself plenty of time to get there. Plan to arrive somewhat ahead of the scheduled time, particularly if your appointment is in the fore part of the day. If a previous candidate fails to appear, the board might be ready for you a bit early. By early afternoon an oral board is almost invariably behind schedule if there are many candidates, and you may have to wait. Take along a book or magazine to read, or your application to review, but leave any extraneous material in the waiting room when you go in for your interview. In any event, relax and compose yourself.

The matter of dress is important. The board is forming impressions about you – from your experience, your manners, your attitude, and your appearance. Give your personal appearance careful attention. Dress your best, but not your flashiest. Choose conservative, appropriate clothing, and be sure it is immaculate. This is a business interview, and your appearance should indicate that you regard it as such. Besides, being well groomed and properly dressed will help boost your confidence.

Sooner or later, someone will call your name and escort you into the interview room. *This is it.* From here on you are on your own. It is too late for any more preparation. But remember, you asked for this opportunity to prove your fitness, and you are here because your request was granted.

What happens when you go in?

The usual sequence of events will be as follows: The clerk (who is often the board stenographer) will introduce you to the chairman of the oral board, who will introduce you to the other members of the board. Acknowledge the introductions before you sit down. Do not be surprised if you find a microphone facing you or a stenotypist sitting by. Oral interviews are usually recorded in the event of an appeal or other review.

Usually the chairman of the board will open the interview by reviewing the highlights of your education and work experience from your application – primarily for the benefit of the other members of the board, as well as to get the material into the record. Do not interrupt or comment unless there is an error or significant misinterpretation; if that is the case, do not hesitate. But do not quibble about insignificant matters. Also, he will usually ask you some question about your education, experience or your present job – partly to get you to start talking and to establish the interviewing "rapport." He may start the actual questioning, or turn it over to one of the other members. Frequently, each member undertakes the questioning on a particular area, one in which he is perhaps most competent, so you can expect each member to participate in the examination. Because time is limited, you may also expect some rather abrupt switches in the direction the questioning takes, so do not be upset by it. Normally, a board member will not pursue a single line of questioning unless he discovers a particular strength or weakness.

After each member has participated, the chairman will usually ask whether any member has any further questions, then will ask you if you have anything you wish to add. Unless you are expecting this question, it may floor you. Worse, it may start you off on an extended, extemporaneous speech. The board is not usually seeking more information. The question is principally to offer you a last opportunity to present further qualifications or to indicate that you have nothing to add. So, if you feel that a significant qualification or characteristic has been overlooked, it is proper to point it out in a sentence or so. Do not compliment the board on the thoroughness of their examination – they have been sketchy, and you know it. If you wish, merely say, "No thank you, I have nothing further to add." This is a point where you can "talk yourself out" of a good impression or fail to present an important bit of information. Remember, *you close the interview yourself.*

The chairman will then say, "That is all, Mr. _____, thank you." Do not be startled; the interview is over, and quicker than you think. Thank him, gather your belongings and take your leave. Save your sigh of relief for the other side of the door.

How to put your best foot forward

Throughout this entire process, you may feel that the board individually and collectively is trying to pierce your defenses, seek out your hidden weaknesses and embarrass and confuse you. Actually, this is not true. They are obliged to make an appraisal of your qualifications for the job you are seeking, and they want to see you in your best light. Remember, they must interview all candidates and a non-cooperative candidate may become a failure in spite of their best efforts to bring out his qualifications. Here are 15 suggestions that will help you:

1) Be natural – Keep your attitude confident, not cocky

If you are not confident that you can do the job, do not expect the board to be. Do not apologize for your weaknesses, try to bring out your strong points. The board is interested in a positive, not negative, presentation. Cockiness will antagonize any board member and make him wonder if you are covering up a weakness by a false show of strength.

2) Get comfortable, but don't lounge or sprawl

Sit erectly but not stiffly. A careless posture may lead the board to conclude that you are careless in other things, or at least that you are not impressed by the importance of the occasion. Either conclusion is natural, even if incorrect. Do not fuss with your clothing, a pencil or an ashtray. Your hands may occasionally be useful to emphasize a point; do not let them become a point of distraction.

3) Do not wisecrack or make small talk

This is a serious situation, and your attitude should show that you consider it as such. Further, the time of the board is limited – they do not want to waste it, and neither should you.

4) Do not exaggerate your experience or abilities

In the first place, from information in the application or other interviews and sources, the board may know more about you than you think. Secondly, you probably will not get away with it. An experienced board is rather adept at spotting such a situation, so do not take the chance.

5) If you know a board member, do not make a point of it, yet do not hide it

Certainly you are not fooling him, and probably not the other members of the board. Do not try to take advantage of your acquaintanceship – it will probably do you little good.

6) Do not dominate the interview

Let the board do that. They will give you the clues – do not assume that you have to do all the talking. Realize that the board has a number of questions to ask you, and do not try to take up all the interview time by showing off your extensive knowledge of the answer to the first one.

7) Be attentive

You only have 20 minutes or so, and you should keep your attention at its sharpest throughout. When a member is addressing a problem or question to you, give him your undivided attention. Address your reply principally to him, but do not exclude the other board members.

8) Do not interrupt

A board member may be stating a problem for you to analyze. He will ask you a question when the time comes. Let him state the problem, and wait for the question.

9) Make sure you understand the question

Do not try to answer until you are sure what the question is. If it is not clear, restate it in your own words or ask the board member to clarify it for you. However, do not haggle about minor elements.

10) Reply promptly but not hastily

A common entry on oral board rating sheets is "candidate responded readily," or "candidate hesitated in replies." Respond as promptly and quickly as you can, but do not jump to a hasty, ill-considered answer.

11) Do not be peremptory in your answers

A brief answer is proper – but do not fire your answer back. That is a losing game from your point of view. The board member can probably ask questions much faster than you can answer them.

12) Do not try to create the answer you think the board member wants

He is interested in what kind of mind you have and how it works – not in playing games. Furthermore, he can usually spot this practice and will actually grade you down on it.

13) Do not switch sides in your reply merely to agree with a board member

Frequently, a member will take a contrary position merely to draw you out and to see if you are willing and able to defend your point of view. Do not start a debate, yet do not surrender a good position. If a position is worth taking, it is worth defending.

14) Do not be afraid to admit an error in judgment if you are shown to be wrong

The board knows that you are forced to reply without any opportunity for careful consideration. Your answer may be demonstrably wrong. If so, admit it and get on with the interview.

15) Do not dwell at length on your present job

The opening question may relate to your present assignment. Answer the question but do not go into an extended discussion. You are being examined for a *new* job, not your present one. As a matter of fact, try to phrase ALL your answers in terms of the job for which you are being examined.

Basis of Rating

Probably you will forget most of these "do's" and "don'ts" when you walk into the oral interview room. Even remembering them all will not ensure you a passing grade. Perhaps you did not have the qualifications in the first place. But remembering them will help you to put your best foot forward, without treading on the toes of the board members.

Rumor and popular opinion to the contrary notwithstanding, an oral board wants you to make the best appearance possible. They know you are under pressure – but they also want to see how you respond to it as a guide to what your reaction would be under the pressures of the job you seek. They will be influenced by the degree of poise you display, the personal traits you show and the manner in which you respond.

ABOUT THIS BOOK

This book contains tests divided into Examination Sections. Go through each test, answering every question in the margin. We have also attached a sample answer sheet at the back of the book that can be removed and used. At the end of each test look at the answer key and check your answers. On the ones you got wrong, look at the right answer choice and learn. Do not fill in the answers first. Do not memorize the questions and answers, but understand the answer and principles involved. On your test, the questions will likely be different from the samples. Questions are changed and new ones added. If you understand these past questions you should have success with any changes that arise. Tests may consist of several types of questions. We have additional books on each subject should more study be advisable or necessary for you. Finally, the more you study, the better prepared you will be. This book is intended to be the last thing you study before you walk into the examination room. Prior study of relevant texts is also recommended. NLC publishes some of these in our Fundamental Series. Knowledge and good sense are important factors in passing your exam. Good luck also helps. So now study this Passbook, absorb the material contained within and take that knowledge into the examination. Then do your best to pass that exam.

EXAMINATION SECTION

EXAMINATION SECTION
TEST 1

DIRECTIONS: Each question or incomplete statement is followed by several suggested answers or completions. Select the one that BEST answers the question or completes the statement. *PRINT THE LETTER OF THE CORRECT ANSWER IN THE SPACE AT THE RIGHT.*

1. As a superior officer, you have the responsibility of deciding whether some of your duties should be delegated to subordinate officers.
   The delegation of certain duties to subordinates is GENERALLY considered

   A. *inadvisable;* subordinates should not share your responsibilities
   B. *advisable;* this will help to prevent you from getting bogged down with minor details and problems
   C. *inadvisable;* you can probably do all parts of your job better than anyone else can
   D. *advisable;* more time can therefore be devoted to day-to-day operations and less to long-range planning

2. Assume that you are a superior officer and that one of your subordinates is careless in the performance of his job.
   Of the following, it would be MOST important for you, when helping this employee, to realize that

   A. punitive methods produce better long-term results than non-punitive methods
   B. most problem officers require strict supervision rather than counseling and training
   C. the superior can often play a large part in changing employee patterns of work
   D. if orders are given in detail, carelessness will be eliminated

3. One of the key qualities of a good superior officer is his ability to balance his work load against the time available to him to complete the job.
   Of the following, the BEST procedure for a superior to follow in establishing his work priorities is to

   A. organize tasks according to urgency without regard to importance
   B. undertake all important, difficult tasks in any order and delegate the routine work to subordinates
   C. assign all work to various subordinates and guide their handling of the problems
   D. delegate those problems that can be solved by others and personally handle the difficult, most pressing issues first

4. It is generally CORRECT to state that the planning process within an organization

   A. is a management responsibility and should not involve the participation of operating personnel
   B. should include long-range programs and goals, and should not include activities which can be carried out within a few weeks or months
   C. is to be used in order to develop and improve practices and procedures but is not to be used in applying these procedures in actual operations
   D. should be used at all supervisory levels since each superior officer must determine how to accomplish tasks and what resources are needed

1.____

2.____

3.____

4.____

5. Assume you are a superior officer and one of your subordinates, who has a low performance rating, has made a good suggestion that will make his job easier.
The BEST course of action for you to take in this situation is to

   A. disregard his suggestion, since he is only trying to do as little work as possible
   B. use his suggestion, since it is a positive suggestion and could motivate him to do better work
   C. use his suggestion, but transfer him to a position where he will not benefit from it
   D. disregard his suggestion, and have a talk with him about his poor performance

6. The use of different criteria to rate employees in different jobs is GENERALLY considered

   A. *desirable,* chiefly because people should be treated as individuals with varying strengths and weaknesses
   B. *undesirable,* chiefly because the use of different criteria results in unfair evaluations
   C. *desirable,* chiefly because people in different jobs cannot always be rated on the basis of the same criteria
   D. *undesirable,* chiefly because ratings that are standardized cannot be compared

7. In preparing an annual division budget for equipment and supplies, the one of the following methods that is MOST appropriate to use is to

   A. combine the previous year's division budget with the estimate of any additional or reduced needs for the coming year
   B. determine what amount the department will approve and use that figure
   C. overestimate division needs by 10% because the department will automatically reduce the figure that is first submitted
   D. underestimate division needs because a reduction in the budget indicates increased efficiency

8. All of the following are objectives of in-service training EXCEPT

   A. discovering and developing skills
   B. providing better service to the public
   C. raising the status of the service
   D. eliminating the need for performance evaluations

9. From a management point of view, the one of the following that is the MOST important advantage of regular personnel performance appraisals is that they

   A. help an officer to prepare for promotion examinations
   B. pinpoint an officer's personality weaknesses
   C. provide an opportunity for regular discussions, including counseling, between an officer and his superior
   D. provide the setting to explain the reasons for disciplinary actions which an officer might not understand

10. Assume that an officer arrests a man for assaulting a woman in the building he is guarding. Later, while the suspect is being searched, the officer finds a switchblade knife, four bags of heroin, and three hypodermic syringes in his clothing.
In these circumstances, the possession of which of the following items might indicate a violation of some law?

    A. Only the heroin
    B. The heroin, the hypodermic syringes, but not the switchblade knife
    C. The switchblade knife, the heroin, but not the hypodermic syringes
    D. The switchblade knife, the heroin, and the hypodermic syringes

11. Upon arriving at the scene of a serious crime, a superior officer SHOULD instruct his subordinates to

    A. protect the crime scene
    B. collect, mark, and evaluate evidence
    C. brief the news media on the status of the crime
    D. prevent medical personnel from entering the crime scene

12. In standard police terminology, the term *fugitive warrant* refers to

    A. any type of warrant that is not a local warrant
    B. a written request for the detention of a suspect
    C. a warrant for a person who leaves his local jurisdiction and commits an offense in another jurisdiction
    D. a type of booking made when a person wanted by an out-of-state jurisdiction is arrested by local officers

13. The one of the following actions with respect to an offender that an officer should NOT take when an infraction has been committed is to

    A. inform the offender of his rights
    B. punish the offender
    C. warn the offender of possible consequences
    D. apprehend the offender using appropriate force

14. Perimeter barriers, intrusion devices, protective lighting, and a personnel identification system are used for good physical security of a building.
An objective of personnel identification and control is to

    A. exempt authorized personnel from compliance with annoying entry and departure procedures
    B. detect unauthorized persons who attempt to gain entry
    C. eliminate the need for expensive perimeter barriers and intrusion alarms
    D. allow an increased number of gates and perimeter entrances to be operated at the same time during peak activity hours

15. A true copy of the testimony taken in a criminal action is known as a(n)

    A. verdict   B. transcript
    C. judgment   D. indictment

16. The process of gathering information during an investigation usually involves interviewing or interrogating witnesses.
Interviews or interrogations are *primarily* used for all of the following purposes EXCEPT to

    A. establish the facts of a possible crime to provide the investigator with leads
    B. verify information already known to the police
    C. secure evidence that may establish the guilt or complicity of a suspect
    D. prevent the person questioned from giving an account of the incident under investigation to newspapers

17. Of the following, the BEST reason to apprehend a narcotics violator out of view of the public is to

    A. prevent the drug user from becoming violent
    B. allow the suspect to *save face* with his friends
    C. prevent the knowledge of his apprehension from reaching any collaborators
    D. keep the suspect from disposing of evidence

18. Assume that you, a superior officer, are planning the physical security operation at a facility. One of the problems you are faced with is that of casual thievery by staff.
Of the following, the BEST means of discouraging such thievery is by establishing

    A. an aggressive security education program
    B. adequate inventory control measures
    C. spot search procedures
    D. an effective key control system

19. Under an officer's scope of authority, all of the following actions would be proper EXCEPT

    A. apprehending persons attempting to gain unauthorized access to any work location
    B. enforcing the traffic control rules applicable to the work location
    C. removing persons suspected of theft with a warning to them not to return
    D. responding to protective alarm signals and other warning devices

20. One of the ways of deploying an officer force at the scene of a demonstration is called *strength in reserve*. This procedure involves having only a few officers police the demonstration while most are being held in reserve. Which one of the following is a DISADVANTAGE of this type of deployment?
It

    A. permits the demonstrators to estimate the number of officers available
    B. might result in a delay between a violent outbreak and the arrival of enough officers to handle the situation
    C. prevents the superior officer from deploying his forces
    D. does not permit rotation of the officers confronting the demonstrators

21. Of the following, the MOST important principle to keep in mind when making arrests is that 21.____

    A. the absence of force will discourage resistance on the part of the offender
    B. the arresting officer should assume, for his own safety, that the person to be arrested is dangerous
    C. once the offender is arrested he should be kept at the scene of the arrest and questioned
    D. in order to prevent violence, it is better to have too few officers making arrests than too many

22. Of the following steps, the one that an officer should take FIRST upon discovering a broken electrical power line while on duty is to 22.____

    A. notify his supervisor
    B. notify the electrical company
    C. determine whether it is a live wire
    D. take measures to protect and barricade the area

23. Assume you are a superior officer interrogating a suspect. The FIRST question you ask him should usually pertain to 23.____

    A. his name and address
    B. a package which he may be carrying
    C. where he has been
    D. where he is going

24. Which one of the following statements concerning the interrogation of a juvenile is INCORRECT? 24.____

    A. The juvenile should be advised of his rights.
    B. The juvenile should be told as little as possible about the case.
    C. A bond of mutual interest should be established with the juvenile.
    D. The juvenile should be encouraged to ask the interrogator questions.

25. Assume that an intoxicated man has wandered into a center and is begging for money and harassing clients. Of the following, the MOST effective action to take in this situation would be to 25.____

    A. call immediately for police assistance
    B. take the man aside quietly and try to persuade him to move along
    C. ask two or three male clients to help you take the man outside
    D. arrest the man at once so that drunks will know they should stay away

KEY (CORRECT ANSWERS)

1. B	11. A
2. C	12. D
3. D	13. B
4. D	14. B
5. B	15. B
6. C	16. D
7. A	17. C
8. D	18. C
9. C	19. C
10. D	20. B

21. B
22. D
23. A
24. D
25. B

TEST 2

DIRECTIONS: Each question or incomplete statement is followed by several suggested answers or completions. Select the one that BEST answers the question or completes the statement. *PRINT THE LETTER OF THE CORRECT ANSWER IN THE SPACE AT THE RIGHT.*

1. Assume that you, a superior officer, have received a communication from one of your subordinates that his center has just received a *ticking* package.
   Of the following steps, the one that he should take FIRST is to

   A. notify the Police Department
   B. remove the package and soak it in water
   C. check the contents of the package
   D. evacuate the area

2. Assume that an individual suspected of drug abuse is apprehended. The suspect produces a prescription which he claims is for the drug found on his person.
   Which of the following actions should be taken NEXT?

   A. The prescription should be disregarded and the suspect should be arrested.
   B. Release the individual, but confiscate the drug in order to have a laboratory check its composition.
   C. The opinion of a medical doctor should be obtained.
   D. The suspect should be released since he has a prescription.

3. A mob has been defined as a group of individuals who commit lawless acts under the stimulus of intense excitement or agitation.
   All of the following are generally considered characteristics of a mob EXCEPT

   A. some degree of organization
   B. one or more leaders
   C. a common motive for action
   D. unemotional behavior

4. Which of the following would be IMPROPER for an officer to do while apprehending a suspect?

   A. Maintain a quiet voice and manner
   B. Remove the person from the scene as soon as possible in order to avoid conflict with the suspect and bystanders
   C. Allow the suspect to realize that the officer does not like persons who commit crimes
   D. Direct and accompany the person to an appropriate location

5. Which of the following is MOST appropriate for an officer to do while testifying as a witness in court?

   A. State the facts only of your own knowledge
   B. Argue with the defense attorney in order to show that your actions were proper
   C. Deny that you have discussed the case outside of court even if you have done so only with close friends
   D. Use as much technical language as possible in order to impress the jury with your knowledge

6. It is sometimes inadvisable to arrest the leaders of an unlawful demonstration immediately.
Of the following, the BEST reason to delay arresting the leaders of a demonstration is to

   A. permit them to restrain their followers who might threaten violence
   B. avoid unfavorable coverage by the press
   C. determine whether there is more than one charge involved
   D. let them get deeper in trouble so they will receive longer sentences when convicted

7. The one of the following approaches which would BEST foster good human relations when dealing with the public is for an officer to

   A. act very self-assured, thus gaining respect
   B. learn how to appeal to the biases and prejudices of others
   C. treat everyone in exactly the same way since everyone has the same needs
   D. appeal to the positive interests of others

8. The causes of many job complaints come not just from wages and working conditions but also from contacts with people on and off the job and from the officer's background and outlook on life.
Because of this, the BEST of the following ways for a superior officer to handle a complaint from a subordinate is generally to

   A. talk to the officer for the purpose of getting him to withdraw his complaint
   B. get as much information as possible to try to determine the real causes of the complaint
   C. postpone action on the complaint since conditions change so rapidly that it is useless to try to act quickly on a complaint
   D. handle each complaint as quickly as possible without looking into the motives for the complaint

9. In every unit certain officers are more cooperative than others.
The one of the following that is MOST likely to occur with regard to supervising such cooperative officers is that they

   A. are more easily intimidated
   B. are often assigned to difficult jobs
   C. are unfriendly to the general public
   D. assume a supervisor's position in dealing with others

10. Assume that you are a superior officer and that one of your subordinate officers comes to you with a complaint about an officer under his command. After listening to a few of the details, you suspect that his complaint is not justified.
Considering this, you should do all of the following during this initial conversation EXCEPT

    A. listen with interest until the subordinate officer finishes making his complaint
    B. tell the subordinate officer that you will investigate the matter further
    C. inform the subordinate that his complaint is invalid
    D. ask the subordinate officer further questions about his complaint

11. As a superior officer, you may receive complaints about the department or individual officers from the public.
    Of the following, the PROPER attitude to take with regard to such complaints is that they

    A. are often helpful in determining how to give the public better service
    B. cause poor morale in the service and should not be revealed to subordinates
    C. are useful as a basis for disciplining officers who have been troublesome in the past
    D. take up too much of an officer's time and should not be accepted

12. One of the people present at a local parent-teacher organization meeting complained about the time it took for him to be taken care of at an agency office. A superior officer, present at the meeting, stood up and explained to the person and the group that there was no personal discrimination involved because the normal procedures took a while and that everyone spent about the same amount of time in the office.
    In this situation, the action of the superior officer was

    A. *proper,* mainly because it will show the group how much he knows about agency operations
    B. *improper,* mainly because he should tell the man who complained to check first with the agency before complaining
    C. *proper,* mainly because he helped to clear up a misunderstanding
    D. *improper,* mainly because the officer should not discuss his agency in public

13. Assume that you are a superior officer and that you have begun a campaign to encourage your subordinates to be prompt in reporting for work. One of your subordinates requests that he be allowed to arrive a half hour late in the morning while his wife is in the hospital as a maternity patient.
    Of the following actions, it would be BEST in this situation for you to

    A. *refuse* the request, claiming it would be unfair to others to make an exception
    B. *grant* the request, telling your other subordinates the reason for this exception
    C. *refuse* the request, blaming the central office for having inflexible rules
    D. *grant* the request, making it clear to all that this will be the last exception

14. Authorities agree that keeping rumors to a minimum is one of the goals of communication.
    Which of the following is NOT consistent with this goal?

    A. Distribute information that will tend to make rumors unnecessary
    B. Reduce the social distance between top management and the lower supervisors
    C. Stress the development of downward rather than upward channels of communication
    D. Understand the emotional elements that cause stress

15. Of the following, the MOST important factor in determining the success or failure of communication between officers and the public is the

    A. attitude of the public toward the officers prior to and during the communication
    B. use of proper channels of communication within the organization
    C. use of the mass media to change the public's attitude from negative to positive
    D. increase in opportunities for personal contact between the officers and the public

16. Assume that you are a superior officer concerned with the effective use of praise and criticism to motivate your subordinates.
Of the following statements, the one that is EQUALLY TRUE of praise and criticism is that both should generally be

    A. directed mainly toward the act instead of the person
    B. given often and with no restrictions
    C. given in public for the greatest effect
    D. directed toward group efforts rather than individual efforts

17. Which of the following actions on the part of a superior officer is MOST likely to improve upward communication between his subordinates and himself?

    A. Delay acting on undesirable working conditions until complaints from subordinates have reached top management
    B. Make the time to listen to subordinates' ideas
    C. Resist becoming involved with the personal problems of subordinates
    D. Discourage communications that indicate which policies may have resulted in poor performance

18. Assume that you are a recently appointed superior officer and are told that one of your subordinates is a chronic complainer.
In this situation, which of the following steps should you take FIRST?

    A. Report your subordinate to higher authority
    B. Discipline your subordinate for his poor performance
    C. Change your subordinate's tour of duty
    D. Ask your subordinate for a list of his complaints

19. In addition to formal supervision, every group of officers soon develops informal leaders who influence the other members of the group.
Of the following statements about informal leaders, the one that is GENERALLY correct is that they

    A. provide supervision when the regular supervisor is absent
    B. are entitled to special benefits for their services
    C. can be used to help settle disputes between employees
    D. prevent the rapid transmission of orders

20. The grapevine is a frequently used means of informal communication in any work location.
The one of the following statements that BEST describes the attitude a superior officer should take in relation to the grapevine is that it is

    A. unreliable and should not be trusted
    B. useful and should be recognized
    C. valuable and should be the chief method of transmitting orders
    D. insignificant and should be ignored

21. As a supervising officer, it may be useful for you to conduct periodic interviews with each of your subordinates to discuss his job performance in broad perspective.
All of the following are ground rules to follow during such an interview EXCEPT

   A. showing him how he compares in work performance with other supervisors in your district
   B. giving him a chance to talk
   C. focusing on what can be learned from any mistakes discussed rather than on the mistakes themselves
   D. avoiding a discussion of personalities

22. When you, as a superior officer, are correcting the errors of a supervisor in your district, which of the following is NOT a good point to keep in mind?

   A. Find something on which to compliment the supervisor before you correct him
   B. Watch yourself carefully to avoid the mistake of overcorrecting
   C. Correct the supervisor at the same time as you correct other supervisors who make similar mistakes
   D. Induce the supervisor to correct himself if possible

23. Following are four steps to be used when instructing a subordinate in the performance of his job:
   I. Observe the subordinate doing the job
   II. Compare his performance to established standards
   III. Explain the purpose of the job to the subordinate
   IV. Demonstrate each step of the job

   Which of the following choices lists the CORRECT order in which the above steps should be taken?

   A. III, IV, I, II
   B. IV, III, I, II
   C. III, IV, II, I
   D. IV, III, II, I

24. Of the following leadership characteristics, the one that is generally considered PRIMARY for a supervisor is the ability to

   A. achieve good working relations with fellow supervisors
   B. get subordinates to air their personal problems
   C. take action to get the job done
   D. plan his work efficiently

25. A recently appointed supervising officer is placed in charge of a district which includes several senior employees. He finds that while these subordinates are able to learn new tasks and methods, some of them tend to take longer to learn procedural changes than newer, younger workers.
Of the following, the MAIN reason for this is that senior workers

   A. are embarrassed by younger workers' intelligence
   B. have to *unlearn* what was taught them in the past
   C. form learning blocks when they are supervised by a younger person
   D. are more interested in doing the work than in academic discussion

KEY (CORRECT ANSWERS)

1.	D	11.	A
2.	C	12.	C
3.	D	13.	B
4.	C	14.	C
5.	A	15.	A
6.	A	16.	A
7.	D	17.	B
8.	B	18.	D
9.	B	19.	C
10.	C	20.	B
21.	A		
22.	C		
23.	A		
24.	C		
25.	B		

EXAMINATION SECTION
TEST 1

DIRECTIONS: Each question or incomplete statement is followed by several suggested answers or completions. Select the one that BEST answers the question or completes the statement. *PRINT THE LETTER OF THE CORRECT ANSWER IN THE SPACE AT THE RIGHT.*

1. Of the following, the MOST important single factor in any building security program is 1.____

    A. a fool-proof employee identification system
    B. an effective control of entrances and exits
    C. bright illumination of all outside areas
    D. clearly marking public and non-public areas

2. There is general agreement that the BEST criterion of what is a good physical security system in a large public building is 2.____

    A. the number of uniformed officers needed to patrol sensitive areas
    B. how successfully the system prevents rather than detects violations
    C. the number of persons caught in the act of committing criminal offenses
    D. how successfully the system succeeds in maintaining good public relations

3. Which one of the following statements most correctly expresses the CHIEF reason why women were originally made eligible for appointment to the position of officer? 3.____

    A. Certain tasks in security protection can be performed best by assigning women.
    B. More women than men are available to fill many vacancies in this position.
    C. The government wants more women in law enforcement because of their better attendance records.
    D. Women can no longer be barred from any government jobs because of sex.

4. The MOST BASIC purpose of patrol by officers is to 4.____

    A. eliminate as much as possible the opportunity for successful misconduct
    B. investigate criminal complaints and accident cases
    C. give prompt assistance to employees and citizens in distress or requesting their help
    D. take persons into custody who commit criminal offenses against persons and property

5. The highest quality of patrol service is MOST generally obtained by 5.____

    A. frequently changing the post assignments of each officer
    B. assigning officers to posts of equal size
    C. assigning problem officers to the least desirable posts
    D. assigning the same officers to the same posts

6. The one of the following requirements which is MOST essential to the successful performance of patrol duty by individual officers is their 6.____

    A. ability to communicate effectively with higher-level officers
    B. prompt signalling according to a prescribed schedule to insure post coverages at all times

13

C. knowledge of post conditions and post hazards
D. willingness to cover large areas during periods of critical manpower shortages

7. Officers on patrol are constantly warned to be on the alert for suspicious persons, actions, and circumstances.
   With this in mind, a senior officer should emphasize the need for them to

   A. be cautious and suspicious when dealing officially with any civilian regardless of the latter's overt actions or the circumstances surrounding his dealings with the police
   B. keep looking for the unusual persons, actions, and circumstances on their posts and pay less attention to the usual
   C. take aggressive police action immediately against any unusual person or condition detected on their posts, regardless of any other circumstances
   D. become thoroughly familiar with the usual on their posts so as to be better able to detect the unusual

8. Of primary importance in the safeguarding of property from theft is a good central lock and key issuance and control system.
   Which one of the following recommendations about maintaining such a control system would be LEAST acceptable?

   A. In selecting locks to be used for the various gates, building, and storage areas, consideration should be given to the amount of security desired.
   B. Master keys should have no markings that will identify them as such and the list of holders of these keys should be frequently reviewed to determine the continuing necessity for the individuals having them.
   C. Whenever keys for outside doors or gates or for other doors which permit access to important buildings and areas are misplaced, the locks should be immediately changed or replaced pending an investigation.
   D. Whenever an employee fails to return a borrowed key at the time specified, a prompt investigation should be made by the security force.

9. In a crowded building, a fire develops in the basement, and smoke enters the crowded rooms on the first floor. Of the following, the BEST action for an officer to take after an alarm is turned in is to

   A. call out a warning that the building is on fire and that everyone should evacuate because of the immediate danger
   B. call all of the officers together for an emergency meeting and discuss a plan of action
   C. immediately call for assistance from the local police station to help in evacuating the crowd
   D. tell everyone that there is a fire in the building next door and that they should move out onto the streets through available exits

10. Which of the following is in a key position to carry out successfully a safety program of an agency? The

    A. building engineer
    B. bureau chiefs
    C. immediate supervisors
    D. public relations director

11. It is GENERALLY considered that a daily roll call inspection, which checks to see that the officers and their equipment are in good order, is   11._____

    A. *desirable,* chiefly because it informs the superior officer what men will have to purchase new uniforms within a month
    B. *desirable,* chiefly because the public forms their impressions of the organization from the appearance of the officers
    C. *undesirable,* chiefly because this kind of daily inspection unnecessarily delays officers in getting to their assigned patrol posts
    D. *undesirable,* chiefly because roll call inspection usually misses individuals reporting to work late

12. A supervising officer in giving instructions to a group of officers on the principles of accident investigation remarked, "A conclusion that appears reasonable will often be changed by exploring a factor of apparently little importance".   12._____
    Which one of the following precautions does this statement emphasize as MOST important in any accident investigation?

    A. Every accident clue should be fully investigated.
    B. Accidents should not be too promptly investigated.
    C. Only specially trained officers should investigate accidents.
    D. Conclusions about accident causes are highly unreliable.

13. On a rainy day, a senior officer found that 9 of his 50 officers reported to work. What percentage of his officers was ABSENT?   13._____

    A. 18%   B. 80%   C. 82%   D. 90%

14. Officer A and Officer B work at the same post on the same days, but their hours are different. Officer A comes to work at 9:00 A.M. and leaves at 5:00 P.M., with a lunch period between 12:15 P.M. and 1:15 P.M. Officer B comes to work at 10:50 A.M. and works until 6:50 P.M., and he takes an hour for lunch between 3:00 P.M. and 4:00 P.M. What is the total amount of time between 9:00 A.M. and 6:50 P.M. that only ONE officer will be on duty?   14._____

    A. 4 hours   B. 4 hours and 40 minutes
    C. 5 hours   D. 5 hours and 40 minutes

15. An officer's log recorded the following attendance of 30 officers: 15._____

    | Monday | 20 | present; | 10 | absent |
    | Tuesday | 28 | present; | 2 | absent |
    | Wednesday | 30 | present; | 0 | absent |
    | Thursday | 21 | present; | 9 | absent |
    | Friday | 16 | present; | 14 | absent |
    | Saturday | 11 | present; | 19 | absent |
    | Sunday | 14 | present; | 16 | absent |

    On the average, how many men were present on the weekdays (Monday - Friday)?

    A. 21   B. 23   C. 25   D. 27

16. An angry woman is being questioned by an officer when she begins shouting abuses at him.
The BEST of the following procedures for the officer to follow is to

   A. leave the room until she has cooled off
   B. politely ignore anything she says
   C. place her under arrest by handcuffing her to a fixed object
   D. warn her that he will have to use force to restrain her making remarks

17. Of the following, which is NOT a recommended practice for an officer placing a woman offender under arrest?

   A. Assume that the offender is an innocent and virtuous person and treat her accordingly.
   B. Protect himself from attack by the woman.
   C. Refrain from using excessive physical force on the offender.
   D. Make the public aware that he is not abusing the woman.

Questions 18-21.

DIRECTIONS: Questions 18 through 21 are to be answered SOLELY on the basis of the following passage.

Specific measures for prevention of pilferage will be based on careful analysis of the conditions at each agency. The most practical and effective method to control casual pilferage is the establishment of psychological deterrents.

One of the most common means of discouraging casual pilferage is to search individuals leaving the agency at unannounced times and places. These spot searches may occasionally detect attempts at theft but greater value is realized by bringing to the attention of individuals the fact that they may be apprehended if they do attempt the illegal removal of property.

An aggressive security education program is an effective means of convincing employees that they have much more to lose than they do to gain by engaging in acts of theft. It is important for all employees to realize that pilferage is morally wrong no matter how insignificant the value of the item which is taken. In establishing any deterrent to casual pilferage, security officers must not lose sight of the fact that most employees are honest and disapprove of thievery. Mutual respect between security personnel and other employees of the agency must be maintained if the facility is to be protected from other more dangerous forms of human hazards. Any security measure which infringes on the human rights or dignity of others will jeopardize, rather than enhance, the overall protection of the agency.

18. The $100,000 yearly inventory of an agency revealed that $50 worth of goods had been stolen; the only individuals with access to the stolen materials were the employees. Of the following measures, which would the author of the preceding paragraph MOST likely recommend to a security officer?

   A. Conduct an intensive investigation of all employees to find the culprit.
   B. Make a record of the theft, but take no investigative or disciplinary action against any employee.
   C. Place a tight security check on all future movements of personnel.
   D. Remove the remainder of the material to an area with much greater security.

19. What does the passage imply is the percentage of employees whom a security officer should expect to be honest?

   A. No employee can be expected to be honest all of the time
   B. Just 50%
   C. Less than 50%
   D. More than 50%

20. According to the passage, the security officer would use which of the following methods to minimize theft in buildings with many exits when his staff is very small?

   A. Conduct an inventory of all material and place a guard near that which is most likely to be pilfered.
   B. Inform employees of the consequences of legal prosecution for pilfering.
   C. Close off the unimportant exits and have all his men concentrate on a few exits.
   D. Place a guard at each exit and conduct a casual search of individuals leaving the premises.

21. Of the following, the title BEST suited for this passage is:

   A. Control Measures for Casual Pilfering
   B. Detecting the Potential Pilferer
   C. Financial losses Resulting from Pilfering
   D. The Use of Moral Persuasion in Physical Security

22. Of the following first aid procedures, which will cause the GREATEST harm in treating a fracture?

   A. Control hemorrhages by applying direct pressure
   B. Keep the broken portion from moving about
   C. Reset a protruding bone by pressing it back into place
   D. Treat the suffering person for shock

23. During a snowstorm, a man comes to you complaining of frostbitten hands. PROPER first aid treatment in this case is to

   A. place the hands under hot running water
   B. place the hands in lukewarm water
   C. call a hospital and wait for medical aid
   D. rub the hands in melting snow

24. While on duty, an officer sees a woman apparently in a state of shock. Of the following, which one is NOT a symptom of shock?

   A. Eyes lacking luster
   B. A cold, moist forehead
   C. A shallow, irregular breathing
   D. A strong, throbbing pulse

25. You notice a man entering your building who begins coughing violently, has shortness of breath, and complains of severe chest pains.
    These symptoms are GENERALLY indicative of

   A. a heart attack   B. a stroke
   C. internal bleeding   D. an epileptic seizure

26. When an officer is required to record the rolled fingerprint impressions of a prisoner on the standard fingerprint form, the technique recommended by the F.B.I. as MOST likely to result in obtaining clear impressions is to roll

 A. all fingers away from the center of the prisoner's body
 B. all fingers toward the center of the prisoner's body
 C. the thumbs away from and the other fingers toward the center of the prisoner's body
 D. the thumbs toward and the other fingers away from the center of the prisoner's body

27. The principle which underlies the operation and use of a lie detector machine is that

 A. a person who is not telling the truth will be able to give a consistent story
 B. a guilty mind will unconsciously associate ideas in a very indicative manner
 C. the presence of emotional stress in a person will result in certain abnormal physical reactions
 D. many individuals are not afraid to lie

Questions 28-32.

DIRECTIONS: Questions 28 through 32 are based SOLELY on the following diagram and the paragraph preceding this group of questions. The paragraph will be divided into two statements. Statement one (1) consists of information given to the senior officer by an agency director; *this information will detail the specific security objectives the senior officer has to meet.* Statement two (2) gives the resources available to the senior officer.

NOTE: The questions are correctly answered only when all of the agency's objectives have been met and when the officer has used all his resources efficiently (i.e., to their maximum effectiveness) in meeting these objectives. All X's in the diagram indicate possible locations of officers' posts. Each X has a corresponding number which is to be used when referring to that location.

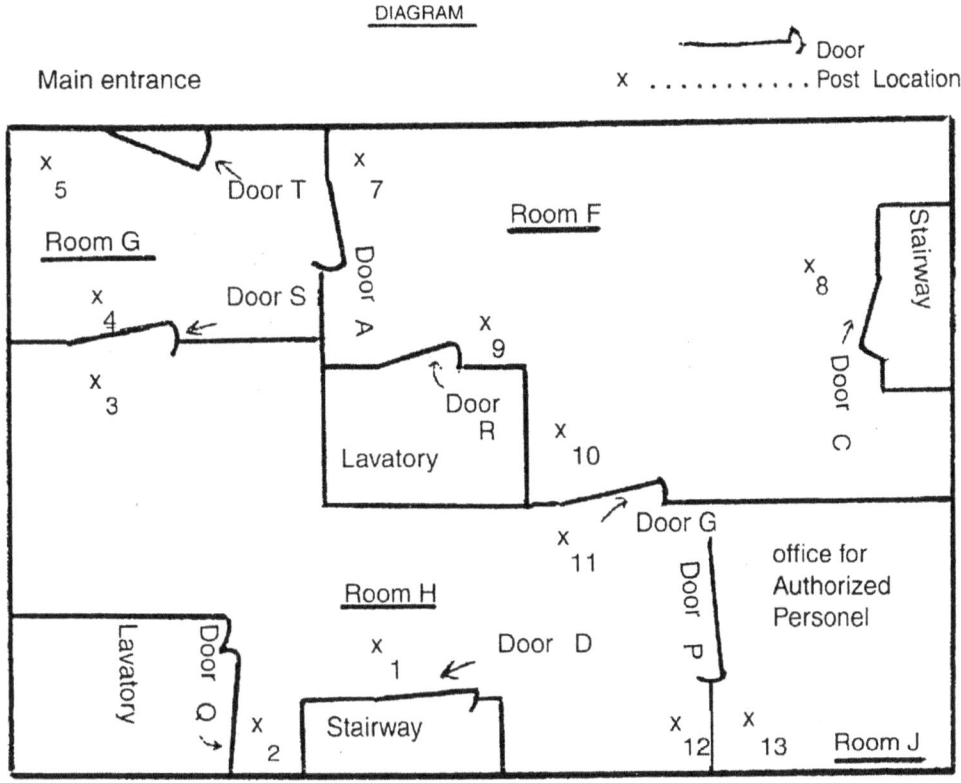

PARAGRAPH

PARAGRAPH

STATEMENT 1: Room G will be the public intake room from which persons will be directed to Room F or Room H; under no circumstances are they to enter the wrong room, and they are not to move from Room F to Room H or vice-versa. A minimum of two officers must be in each room frequented by the public at all times, and they are to keep unauthorized individuals from going to the second floor or into restricted areas. All usable entrances or exits must be covered.

STATEMENT 2: The senior officer can lock any door except the main entrance and stairway doors. He has a staff of five officers to carry out these operations.

NOTE: The senior officer is available for guard duty. Room J is an active office.

28. According to the instructions, how many officers should be assigned inside the office for authorized personnel (Room J)?

    A. 0   B. 1   C. 2   D. 3

28._____

29. In order to keep the public from moving between Room F and Room H, which door(s) can be locked without interfering with normal office operations? Door

    A. G   B. P   C. R and Q   D. S

29._____

30. When placing officers in Room H, the only way the senior officer can satisfy the agency's objectives and his manpower limitations is by placing men at locations

    A. 1 and 3   B. 1 and 12   C. 3 and 11   D. 11 and 12

31. In accordance with the instructions, the LEAST effective locations to place officers in Room F are locations

    A. 7 and 9   B. 7 and 10   C. 8 and 9   D. 9 and 10

32. In which room is it MOST difficult for each of the officers to see all the movements of the public? Room

    A. G   B. F   C. H   D. J

33. According to its own provisions, the Penal Law of the State has a number of general purposes.
    It would be LEAST accurate to state that one of these general purposes is to

    A. give fair warning of the nature of the conduct forbidden and the penalties authorized upon conviction
    B. define the act or omission and accompanying mental state which constitute each offense
    C. regulate the procedure which governs the arrest, trial and punishment of convicted offenders
    D. insure the public safety by preventing the commission of offenses through the deterrent influence of the sentences authorized upon conviction

34. Officers must be well-informed about the meaning of certain terms in connection with their enforcement duties. Which one of the following statements about such terms would be MOST accurate according to the Penal Law of the State? A(n)

    A. offense is always a crime
    B. offense is always a violation
    C. violation is never a crime
    D. felony is never an offense

35. According to the Penal Law of the State, the one of the following elements which must ALWAYS be present in order to justify the arrest of a person for criminal assault is

    A. the infliction of an actual physical injury
    B. an intent to cause an injury
    C. a threat to inflict a physical injury
    D. the use of some kind of weapon

36. A recent law of the State defines who are police officers and who are peace officers. The official title of this law is: The

    A. Criminal Code of Procedure
    B. Law of Criminal Procedure
    C. Criminal Procedure Law
    D. Code of Criminal Procedure

37. If you are required to appear in court to testify as the complainant in a criminal action, it would be MOST important for you to

    A. confine your answers to the questions asked when you are testifying
    B. help the prosecutor even if some exaggeration in your testimony may be necessary
    C. be as fair as possible to the defendant even if some details have to be omitted from your testimony
    D. avoid contradicting other witnesses testifying against the defendant

38. A senior officer is asked by the television news media to explain to the public what happened on his post during an important incident.
    When speaking with departmental permission in front of the tape recorders and cameras, the senior officer can give the MOST favorable impression of himself and his department by

    A. refusing to answer any questions but remaining calm in front of the cameras
    B. giving a detailed report of the wrong decisions made by his agency for handling the particular incident
    C. presenting the appropriate factual information in a competent way
    D. telling what should have been done during the incident and how such incidents will be handled in the future

39. Of the following suggested guidelines for officers, the one which is LEAST likely to be effective in promoting good manners and courtesy in their daily contacts with the public is:

    A. Treat inquiries by telephone in the same manner as those made in person
    B. Never look into the face of the person to whom you are speaking
    C. Never give misinformation in answer to any inquiry on a matter on which you are uncertain of the facts
    D. Show respect and consideration in both trivial and important contacts with the public

40. Assume you are an officer who has had a record of submitting late weekly reports and that you are given an order by your supervisor which is addressed to all line officers. The order states that weekly reports will be replaced by twice-weekly reports.
    The MOST logical conclusion for you to make, of the following, is:

    A. Fully detailed information was missing from your past reports
    B. Most officers have submitted late reports
    C. The supervisor needs more timely information
    D. The supervisor is attempting to punish you for your past late reports

41. A young man with long hair and "mod" clothing makes a complaint to an officer about the rudeness of another officer.
    If the senior officer is not on the premises, the officer receiving the complaint should

    A. consult with the officer who is being accused to see if the youth's story is true
    B. refer the young man to central headquarters
    C. record the complaint made against his fellow officer and ask the youth to wait until he can locate the senior officer
    D. search for the senior officer and bring him back to the site of the complainant

42. During a demonstration, which area should ALWAYS be kept clear of demonstrators?

    A. Water fountains
    B. Seating areas
    C. Doorways
    D. Restrooms

43. During demonstrations, an officer's MOST important duty is to

    A. aid the agency's employees to perform their duties
    B. promptly arrest those who might cause incidents
    C. promptly disperse the crowds of demonstrators
    D. keep the demonstrators from disrupting order

44. Of the following, what is the FIRST action a senior officer should take if a demonstration develops in his area without advance warning?

    A. Call for additional assistance from the police department
    B. Find the leaders of the demonstrators and discuss their demands
    C. See if the demonstrators intend to break the law
    D. Inform his superiors of the event taking place

45. If a senior officer is informed in the morning that a demonstration will take place during the afternoon at his assigned location, he should assemble his officers to discuss the nature and aspects of this demonstration. Of the following, the subject which it is LEAST important to discuss during this meeting is

    A. making a good impression if an officer is called before the television cameras for a personal interview
    B. the known facts and causes of the demonstration
    C. the attitude and expected behavior of the demonstrators
    D. the individual responsibilities of the officers during the demonstration

46. A male officer has probable reason to believe that a group of women occupying the ladies' toilet are using illicit drugs.
    The BEST action, of the following, for the officer to take is to

    A. call for assistance and, with the aid of such assistance, enter the toilet and escort the occupants outside
    B. ignore the situation but recommend that the ladies' toilet be closed temporarily
    C. immediately rush into the ladies' toilet and search the occupants therein
    D. knock on the door of the ladies' toilet and ask their permission to enter so that he will not be accused of trying to molest them

47. Assume that you know that a group of demonstrators will not cooperate with your request to throw handbills in a waste basket instead of on the sidewalk. You ask one of the leaders of the group, who agrees with you, to speak to the demonstrators and ask for their cooperation in this matter.
    Your request of the group leader is

    A. *desirable,* chiefly because an officer needs civilians to control the public since the officer is usually unfriendly to the views of public groups
    B. *undesirable,* chiefly because an officer should never request a civilian to perform his duties
    C. *desirable,* chiefly because the appeal of an acknowledged leader helps in gaining group cooperation

D. *undesirable*, chiefly because an institutional leader is motivated to maneuver a situation to gain his own personal advantage

48. A vague letter received from a female employee in the agency accuses an officer of improper conduct.
The initial investigative interview by the senior officer assigned to check the accusation should GENERALLY be with the

   A. accused officer
   B. female employee
   C. highest superior about disciplinary action against the officer
   D. immediate supervisor of the female employee

48._____

Questions 49-50.

DIRECTIONS: Questions 49 and 50 are to be answered SOLELY on the basis of the information in the following paragraph.

The personal conduct of each member of the Department is the primary factor in promoting desirable police-community relations. Tact, patience, and courtesy shall be strictly observed under all circumstances. A favorable public attitude toward the police must be earned; it is influenced by the personal conduct and attitude of each member of the force, by his personal integrity and courteous manner, by his respect for due process of law, by his devotion to the principles of justice, fairness, and impartiality.

49. According to the preceding paragraph, what is the BEST action an officer can take in dealing with people in a neighborhood?

   A. Assist neighborhood residents by doing favors for them.
   B. Give special attention to the community leaders in order to be able to control them effectively.
   C. Behave in an appropriate manner and give all community members the same just treatment.
   D. Prepare a plan detailing what he, the officer, wants to do for the community and submit it for approval.

49._____

50. As used in the paragraph, the word *impartiality* means *most nearly*

   A. observant   B. unbiased
   C. righteousness   D. honesty

50._____

KEY (CORRECT ANSWERS)

1. B	11. B	21. A	31. D	41. C
2. B	12. A	22. C	32. C	42. C
3. A	13. C	23. B	33. C	43. D
4. A	14. D	24. D	34. C	44. D
5. D	15. B	25. A	35. A	45. A
6. C	16. B	26. D	36. C	46. A
7. D	17. A	27. C	37. A	47. C
8. C	18. B	28. A	38. C	48. B
9. D	19. D	29. A	39. B	49. C
10. C	20. B	30. B	40. C	50. B

TEST 2

DIRECTIONS: Each question or incomplete statement is followed by several suggested answers or completions. Select the one that BEST answers the question or completes the statement. *PRINT THE LETTER OF THE CORRECT ANSWER IN THE SPACE AT THE RIGHT.*

Questions 1-5.

DIRECTIONS: Questions 1 through 5 consist of short paragraphs. Each paragraph contains one word which is INCORRECTLY used because it is NOT in keeping with the meaning of the paragraph. Find the word in each paragraph which is INCORRECTLY used, and then select as the answer the suggested word which should be substituted for the incorrectly used word.

SAMPLE QUESTION

In determining who is to do the work in your unit, you will have to decide just who does what from day to day. One of your lowest responsibilities is to assign work so that everybody gets a fair share and that everyone can do his part well.
   A. new   B. old   C. important   D. performance

EXPLANATION

The word which is NOT in keeping with the meaning of the paragraph is "lowest". This is the INCORRECTLY used word. The suggested word "important" would be in keeping with the meaning of the paragraph and should be substituted for "lowest". Therefore, the CORRECT answer is Choice C.

1. If really good practice in the elimination of preventable injuries is to be achieved and held in any establishment, top management must refuse full and definite responsibility and must apply a good share of its attention to the task.

   A. accept   B. avoidable   C. duties   D. problem

2. Recording the human face for identification is by no means the only service performed by the camera in the field of investigation. When the trial of any issue takes place, a word picture is sought to be distorted to the court of incidents, occurrences, or events which are in dispute.

   A. appeals   B. description
   C. portrayed   D. deranged

3. In the collection of physical evidence, it cannot be emphasized too strongly that a haphazard systematic search at the scene of the crime is vital. Nothing must be overlooked. Often the only leads in a case will come from the results of this search.

   A. important   B. investigation
   C. proof   D. thorough

4. If an investigator has reason to suspect that the witness is mentally stable or a habitual drunkard, he should leave no stone unturned in his investigation to determine if the witness was under the influence of liquor or drugs, or was mentally unbalanced either at the time of the occurrence to which he testified or at the time of the trial.

   A. accused   B. clue   C. deranged   D. question

5. The use of records is a valuable step in crime investigation and is the main reason every department should maintain accurate reports. Crimes are not committed through the use of departmental records alone but from the use of all records, of almost every type, wherever they may be found and whenever they give any incidental information regarding the criminal.

   A. accidental   B. necessary   C. reported   D. solved

Questions 6-8.

DIRECTIONS: Questions 6 through 8 are to be answered SOLELY on the basis of the following passage.

The mass media are an integral part of the daily life of virtually every American. Among these media, the youngest, television, is the most persuasive. Ninety-five percent of American homes have at least one television set, and on the average that set is in use for about 40 hours each week. The central place of television in American life makes this medium the focal point of a growing national concern over the effects of media portrayals of violence on the values, attitudes, and behavior of an ever increasing audience.

In our concern about violence and its causes, it is easy to make television a scapegoat. But we emphasise the fact that there is no simple answer to the problem of violence -- no single explanation of its causes, and no single prescription for its control. It should be remembered that America also experienced high levels of crime and violence in periods before the advent of television.

The problem of balance, taste, and artistic merit in entertaining programs on television are complex. We cannot <u>countenance</u> government censorship of television. Nor would we seek to impose arbitrary limitations on programming which might jeopardize television's ability to deal in dramatic presentations with controversial social issues. Nonetheless, we are deeply troubled by television's constant portrayal of violence, not in any genuine attempt to focus artistic expression on the human condition, but rather in pandering to a public preoccupation with violence that television itself has helped to generate.

6. According to the passage, television uses violence MAINLY

   A. to highlight the reality of everyday existence
   B. to satisfy the audience's hunger for destructive action
   C. to shape the values and attitudes of the public
   D. when it films documentaries concerning human conflict

7. Which one of the following statements is BEST supported by this passage?

   A. Early American history reveals a crime pattern which is not related to television.
   B. Programs should give presentations of social issues and never portray violent acts.
   C. Television has proven that entertainment programs can easily make the balance between taste and artistic merit a simple matter.
   D. Values and behavior should be regulated by governmental censorship.

8. Of the following, which word has the same meaning as <u>countenance</u> as it is used in the above passage?

   A. approve   B. exhibit   C. oppose   D. reject

Questions 9-12.

DIRECTIONS: Questions 9 through 12 are to be answered SOLELY on the basis of the following graph relating to the burglary rate in the city, 2003 to 2008, inclusive.

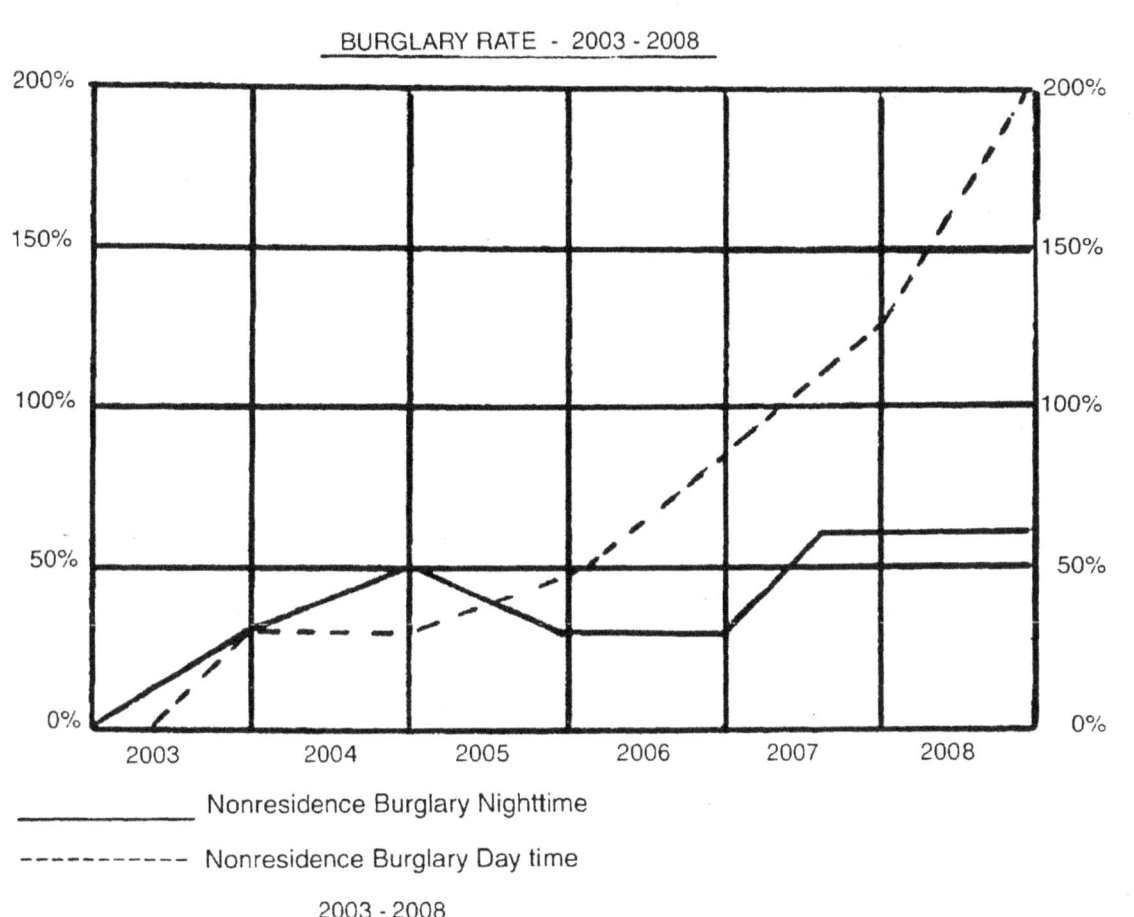

2003 - 2008

9. At the beginning of what year was the percentage increase in daytime and nighttime burglaries the SAME?

   A. 2004   B. 2005   C. 2006   D. 2008

10. In what year did the percentage of nighttime burglaries DECREASE?

   A. 2003   B. 2005   C. 2006   D. 2008

11. In what year was there the MOST rapid increase in the percentage of daytime non-residence burglaries?

   A. 2004   B. 2006   C. 2007   D. 2008

12. At the end of 2007, the actual number of nighttime burglaries committed

   A. was about 20%
   B. was 40%
   C. was 400
   D. cannot be determined from the information given

Questions 13-17.

DIRECTIONS: Questions 13 through 17 consist of two sentences numbered 1 and 2 taken from police officers' reports. Some of these sentences are correct according to ordinary formal English usage. Other sentences are incorrect because they contain errors in English usage or punctuation. Consider a sentence correct if it contains no errors in English usage or punctuation even if there may be other ways of writing the sentence correctly. Mark your answer to each question in the space at the right as follows:
- A. If only sentence 1 is correct, but not sentence 2
- B. If only sentence 2 is correct, but not sentence 1
- C. If sentences 1 and 2 are both correct
- D. If sentences 1 and 2 are both incorrect

SAMPLE QUESTION
1. The woman claimed that the purse was her's.
2. Everyone of the new officers was assigned to a patrol post.

EXPLANATION

Sentence 1 is INCORRECT because of an error in punctuation. The possessive words, "ours, yours, hers, theirs," do not have the apostrophe (').

Sentence 2 is CORRECT because the subject of the sentence is "Everyone" which is singular and requires the singular verb "was assigned".

Since only sentence 2 is correct, but not sentence 1, the CORRECT answer is B.

13.
1. Either the patrolman or his sergeant are always ready to help the public.
2. The sergeant asked the patrolman when he would finish the report.

14.
1. The injured man could not hardly talk.
2. Every officer had ought to hand in their reports on time.

15.
1. Approaching the victim of the assault, two large bruises were noticed by me.
2. The prisoner was arrested for assault, resisting arrest, and use of a deadly weapon.

16.
1. A copy of the orders, which had been prepared by the captain, was given to each patrolman.
2. It's always necessary to inform an arrested person of his constitutional rights before asking him any questions.

17.
1. To prevent further bleeding, I applied a tourniquet tothe wound.
2. John Rano a senior officer was on duty at the time of the accident.

Questions 18-25.

DIRECTIONS: Answer each of Questions 18 through 25 SOLELY on the basis of the statement preceding the questions.

18. The criminal is one whose habits have been erroneously developed or, we should say, developed in anti-social patterns, and therefore the task of dealing with him is not one of punishment, but of treatment.
The basic principle expressed in this statement is BEST illustrated by the

   A. emphasis upon rehabilitation in penal institutions
   B. prevalence of capital punishment for murder
   C. practice of imposing heavy fines for minor violations
   D. legal provision for trial by jury in criminal cases

19. The writ of habeas corpus is one of the great guarantees of personal liberty. Of the following, the BEST justification for this statement is that the writ of habeas corpus is frequently used to

    A. compel the appearance in court of witnesses who are outside the state
    B. obtain the production of books and records at a criminal trial
    C. secure the release of a person improperly held in custody
    D. prevent the use of deception in obtaining testimony of reluctant witnesses

20. Fifteen persons suffered effects of carbon dioxide asphyxiation shortly before noon recently in a seventh-floor pressing shop. The accident occurred in a closed room where six steam presses were in operation. Four men and one woman were overcome.
    Of the following, the MOST probable reason for the fact that so many people were affected simultaneously is that

    A. women evidently show more resistance to the effects of carbon dioxide than men
    B. carbon dioxide is an odorless and colorless gas
    C. carbon dioxide is lighter than air
    D. carbon dioxide works more quickly at higher altitudes

21. Lay the patient on his stomach, one arm extended directly overhead, the other arm bent at the elbow, and with the face turned outward and resting on hand or forearm.
    To the officer who is skilled at administering first aid, these instructions should IMMEDIATELY suggest

    A. application of artificial respiration
    B. treatment for third degree burns of the arm
    C. setting a dislocated shoulder
    D. control of capillary bleeding in the stomach

22. The soda and acid fire extinguisher is the hand extinguisher most commonly used by officers. The main body of the cylinder is filled with a mixture of water and bicarbonate of soda. In a separate interior compartment, at the top, is a small bottle of sulphuric acid. When the extinguisher is inverted, the acid spills into the solution below and starts a chemical reaction. The carbon dioxide thereby generated forces the solution from the extinguisher.
    The officer who understands the operation of this fire extinguisher should know that it is LEAST likely to operate properly

    A. in basements or cellars
    B. in extremely cold weather
    C. when the reaction is of a chemical nature
    D. when the bicarbonate of soda is in solution

23. Suppose that, at a training lecture, you are told that many of the men in our penal institutions today are second and third offenders.
    Of the following, the MOST valid inference you can make SOLELY on the basis of this statement is that

    A. second offenders are not easily apprehended
    B. patterns of human behavior are not easily changed
    C. modern laws are not sufficiently flexible
    D. laws do not breed crimes

24. In all societies of our level of culture, acts are committed which arouse censure severe enough to take the form of punishment by the government. Such acts are crimes, not because of their inherent nature, but because of their ability to arouse resentment and to stimulate repressive measures.
Of the following, the MOST valid inference which can be drawn from this statement is that

    A. society unjustly punishes acts which are inherently criminal
    B. many acts are not crimes but are punished by society because such acts threaten the lives of innocent people
    C. only modern society has a level of culture
    D. societies sometimes disagree as to what acts are crimes

25. Crime cannot be measured directly. Its amount must be inferred from the frequency of some occurrence connected with it; for example, crimes brought to the attention of the police, persons arrested, prosecutions, convictions, and other dispositions, such as probation or commitment. Each of these may be used as an index of the amount of crime. SOLELY on the basis of the foregoing statement, it is MOST correct to state that

    A. the incidence of crime cannot be estimated with any accuracy
    B. the number of commitments is usually greater than the number of probationary sentences
    C. the amount of crime is ordinarily directly correlated with the number of persons arrested
    D. a joint consideration of crimes brought to the attention of the police and the number of prosecutions undertaken gives little indication of the amount of crime in a locality

KEY (CORRECT ANSWERS)

1.	B	11.	D
2.	A	12.	D
3.	D	13.	D
4.	C	14.	D
5.	D	15.	B
6.	B	16.	C
7.	A	17.	A
8.	A	18.	A
9.	A	19.	C
10.	B	20.	B

21. A
22. B
23. B
24. D
25. C

EXAMINATION SECTION
TEST 1

DIRECTIONS: Each question or incomplete statement is followed by several suggested answers or completions. Select the one that BEST answers the question or completes the statement. *PRINT THE LETTER OF THE CORRECT ANSWER IN THE SPACE AT THE RIGHT.*

1. Which of the following is the LEAST important factor to consider in surveying the physical layout of a building for traffic flow?

    A. Location of windows
    B. Number of entrances
    C. Number of exits
    D. Location of first aid rooms

    1._____

2. The major purpose of any security program in a large organization is to prevent unlawful acts.
   If adequate patrol coverage is provided at a given location, it is MOST likely that

    A. crimes will not be committed
    B. undesirables will not enter the building
    C. unlawful acts will increase in the long run
    D. there will be less opportunity to commit a crime

    2._____

3. The MOST frequent cause of fires in public facilities is

    A. incinerators   B. vandalism
    C. electrical sources   D. smoking on the job

    3._____

4. After bomb threats are received, it is sometimes necessary to evacuate a facility. How long BEFORE the threatened time of explosion should a facility be evacuated?
   At least _____ minutes.

    A. 15   B. 25   C. 50   D. 60

    4._____

5. Once a facility is evacuated because of a bomb threat, how much time should pass before the public and employees are allowed to enter the building?
   _____ minutes.

    A. 10   B. 20   C. 40   D. 60

    5._____

6. Of the following locations in public buildings, the one which is the LEAST likely place for bombs to be planted is in

    A. storerooms   B. bathrooms
    C. cafeterias   D. waste receptacles

    6._____

7. The one of the following that is the surest means of establishing positive identification of someone entering a facility is by

    A. personal recognition   B. I.D. badge
    C. social security card   D. driver's license

    7._____

33

8. The one of the following which most probably would NOT be included in a police record report concerning an incident at a facility is the

   A. name of complainant or injured party
   B. name of the investigating officer
   C. statement of each witness
   D. religion of complainant or injured party

9. Preventing trouble is one of the primary concerns of special officers.
   When dealing with unruly groups of people who threaten to become violent, which of the following is a measure which should NOT be taken?

   A. Maintain close surveillance of such groups
   B. Try to contact the leaders of the group regardless of their militancy
   C. Keep the officer force alerted
   D. Have the officer force deal aggressively with provocations

10. Of the following, the MOST important factor to consider in the deployment of officers dealing with a client population is the officers' ability to

    A. remain calm   B. look stern
    C. evaluate personality D. take a firm stand

11. Assume that an offender is struggling with a group of officers who are trying to arrest him.
    What force, if any, can be used to overcome this resistance?

    A. The amount of force acceptable to the public
    B. The amount of force necessary to restrain the offender and protect the officers
    C. Any amount of force that is acceptable to the officers at the scene
    D. No force may be used until the police arrive

12. Assume that a fire is discovered at your work location. The one of the following actions which would be INAPPROPRIATE for you to take is to

    A. notify the telephone operator
    B. station a reliable person at the entrance
    C. open all windows and doors in the area
    D. start evacuating the area

13. If a person has an object caught in his throat or air passage but is breathing adequately, which one of the following should you do?

    A. Probe for the object
    B. Force him to drink water
    C. Lay him over your arm and slap him between the shoulder blades
    D. Allow him to cough and to assume the position he finds most comfortable

14. The one of the following methods which should NOT be used to report a fire is to

    A. call 911
    B. pull the handle in the red box on the street corner
    C. call the fire department county numbers listed in each county directory
    D. call 411

15. Assume that an officer, alone in a building at night, smells the strong odor of cooking or heating gas. In addition to airing the building and making sure that he is not overcome, it would be BEST for the officer to call

    A. his superior at his home and ask for instructions
    B. for a plumber from the department of public works
    C. 911 for police and fire help
    D. the emergency number at Con Edison

16. Of the following situations, the one that is MOST dangerous for an officer is when he

    A. investigates suspicious persons and circumstances
    B. finds a burglary in progress or pursues burglary suspects
    C. attempts an arrest or finds a robbery in progress
    D. patrols on the overnight shift

17. An officer on security patrol generally should spend MOST of his time

    A. checking doors and locks
    B. helping the public and answering questions
    C. chasing criminals and looking for clues
    D. writing reports on unusual incidents

18. The one of the following that is an ACCEPTABLE way to arrest a person is to

    A. tell him to report to the nearest police precinct
    B. send a summons to his permanent address
    C. tell him in person that he is under arrest
    D. show him handcuffs and ask him to come along

19. A carbon dioxide fire extinguisher is BEST suited for extinguishing _____ fires.

    A. paper   B. rag   C. rubbish   D. grease

20. A pressurized water or soda-acid fire extinguisher is BEST suited for extinguishing _____ fires.

    A. wood
    B. gasoline
    C. electrical
    D. magnesium

21. The one of the following statements that does NOT apply to the use of handcuffs is that they

    A. are used as temporary restraining devices
    B. eliminate the need for vigilance
    C. cannot be opened without keys
    D. are used to secure a violent person

22. The one of the following that is GENERALLY a crime against the person is

    A. trespass   B. burglary   C. robbery   D. arson

23. Of the following, the SAFEST way of escape from an office in a burning building is generally the

    A. stairway
    B. rooftop
    C. passenger elevator
    D. freight elevator

24. In attempting to control a possible riot situation, an officer pushed his way into a crowd gathered outside the building and tried to cause confusion by arguing with members of the group.
    This procedure NORMALLY is considered

    A. *desirable;* any violence that occurs will remain outside the building
    B. *desirable;* the crowd will break into smaller groups and disperse
    C. *undesirable;* to maintain control of the situation, the officer must not become part of the crowd
    D. *undesirable;* the supervisor should stay clear of the scene

25. Which one of the following is MOST effective in making officers more safety-minded?

    A. Maintaining an up-to-date library of the latest safety literature
    B. Reading daily safety bulletins at roll-call
    C. Holding informal group safety meetings periodically
    D. Offering prizes for good safety slogans and displays

KEY (CORRECT ANSWERS)

1. A		11. B	
2. D		12. C	
3. C		13. D	
4. A		14. D	
5. D		15. D	
6. C		16. C	
7. A		17. A	
8. D		18. C	
9. D		19. D	
10. A		20. A	

21. B
22. C
23. A
24. C
25. C

TEST 2

DIRECTIONS: Each question or incomplete statement is followed by several suggested answers or completions. Select the one that BEST answers the question or completes the statement. *PRINT THE LETTER OF THE CORRECT ANSWER IN THE SPACE AT THE RIGHT.*

1. Assume that an angry crowd of some 75 to 100 people has built up in one of the hallways of a center and that only one superior officer and two subordinate officers are on duty in the building. A glass panel in one of the stairway doors has just been broken under the pressure of the crowd and a bench has been hurled down a flight of stairs. The one of the following actions that the superior officer SHOULD take in this situation is to

    A. push his way into the crowd and try to reason with them
    B. order the two other officers to try to quiet the crowd
    C. call the police on 911 and meet them outside the building
    D. do nothing at this point in order to avoid a riot

    1.____

2. One of the duties and responsibilities of a supervisor is to test the knowledge of the officers concerning their post conditions.
   This should be done if the officer's assignment is

    A. fixed only
    B. roving only
    C. roving only in a troublesome spot
    D. either fixed or roving

    2.____

3. An officer discovers early one morning that an office in the building he guards has been burglarized.
   Of the following, it is important for the officer to FIRST

    A. go through the building and look for suspects
    B. call the police and protect the area and whatever evidence exists until they arrive
    C. allow people into their offices as they come to work
    D. examine, sort, and handle all evidence before the police get there

    3.____

4. Assume that two officers are interrogating one suspect. How should these officers position themselves during the interrogation?

    A. One officer should stand on either side of the suspect.
    B. One officer should stand to the right of the suspect, and the other officer should stand behind the suspect.
    C. Both officers should stand to the right of the suspect.
    D. One officer should stand to the right of the suspect, and the other officer should stand in front of the suspect.

    4.____

5. A witness who takes an oath to testify truly and who states as true any matter which he knows to be false is guilty of

    A. perjury   B. libel   C. slander   D. fraud

    5.____

6. An officer checking a substance suspected of containing narcotics should GENERALLY

   A. taste it in small amounts
   B. send it to a laboratory for analysis
   C. smell it for its distinctive odor
   D. examine it for its unusual texture

7. A certain center is situated in an area where frequent outbreaks of hostilities seem to be focused on the center itself.
   Which of the following BEST explains why the center may be a target for hostile acts?
   It

   A. serves community needs
   B. represents governmental authority
   C. represents all ethnic groups
   D. serves as a neutral battlefield

8. An officer often deals with people who might be addicted to drugs.
   The one of the following symptoms which is NOT generally an indication of drug addiction is

   A. dilation of the eye pupils
   B. frequent yawning and sneezing
   C. a deep, rasping cough
   D. continual itching of the arms and legs

9. In emergency situations, panic will MOST probably occur when people are

   A. unexpectedly confronted with a terrorizing condition from which there appears to be no escape
   B. angry and violent
   C. anxious about circumstances which are not obvious, easily visible or within the immediate area
   D. familiar with the effects of the emergency

10. The one of the following actions on the part of a person that would NOT be considered *resisting arrest* is

    A. retreating and running away
    B. saying, *You can't arrest me*
    C. pushing the officer aside
    D. pulling away from an officer's grasp

11. Which of the following items would NOT be considered an APPROPRIATE item of uniform for an officer to wear while on duty?

    A. Reefer type overcoat
    B. Leather laced shoes with flat soles
    C. White socks
    D. Cap cover with cap device displayed

12. What can happen to an officer if the leather thong on his night stick is NOT twisted correctly?
    The

    A. baton may be taken out of the officer's hand
    B. officer's wrist may be broken
    C. leather will tear more easily
    D. officer's arm may be injured

13. The one of the following kinds of information which SHOULD be included in the log book is

    A. any important matter of police information
    B. an item noted in Standard Operating Procedures only
    C. everything of general interest
    D. a crime or offense only

14. While on patrol at your work location, you receive a call that an assault has taken place. Upon your arrival at the scene, the victim, who has severe lacerations, informs you that the assailant ran into a nearby basement.
    After apprehending the suspect, the type of search you should conduct is a _____ search.

    A. wall   B. frisk   C. body   D. strip

15. A tactical force is valuable in MOST emergency situations PRIMARILY because of its

    A. location   B. morale
    C. flexibility   D. size

16. An officer should be encouraged to talk easily and frankly when he is dealing with his superior.
    In order to encourage such free communication, it would be MOST appropriate for a superior to behave in a(n)

    A. *sincere* manner; assure the officer that you will deal with him honestly and openly
    B. *official* manner; you are a superior officer and must always act formally with subordinates
    C. *investigative* manner; you must probe and question to get to a basis of trust
    D. *unemotional* manner; the officer's emotions and background should play no part in your dealings with him

17. Research findings show that an increase in free communication within an agency GENERALLY results in which one of the following?

    A. Improved morale and productivity
    B. Increased promotional opportunities
    C. An increase in authority
    D. A spirit of honesty

18. Assume that you are a superior officer and your superiors have given you a new arrest procedure to be followed. Before passing this information on to your subordinates, the one of the following actions that you should take FIRST is to

    A. ask your superiors to send out a memorandum to the entire staff
    B. clarify the procedure in your own mind
    C. set up a training course to provide instructions on the new procedure
    D. write a memorandum to your subordinates

19. Communication is necessary for an organization to be effective.
    The one of the following which is LEAST important for most communication systems is that

    A. messages are sent quickly and directly to the person who needs them to operate
    B. information should be conveyed understandably and accurately
    C. the method used to transmit information should be kept secret so that security can be maintained
    D. senders of messages must know how their messages were received and acted upon

20. Which one of the following is the CHIEF advantage of listening willingly to subordinate officers and encouraging them to talk freely and honestly?
    It

    A. reveals to superiors the degree to which ideas that are passed down are accepted by subordinates
    B. reduces the participation of subordinates in the operation of the department
    C. encourages officers to try for promotion
    D. enables officers to learn about security leaks on the part of officials

21. A superior may be informed through either oral or written reports.
    Which one of the following is an ADVANTAGE of using oral reports?

    A. There is no need for a formal record of the report.
    B. An exact duplicate of the report is not easily transmitted to others.
    C. A good oral report requires little time for preparation.
    D. An oral report involves two-way communication between a subordinate and his superior.

22. Of the following, the MOST important reason why officers should communicate effectively with the public is to

    A. improve the public's understanding of information that is important for them to know
    B. establish a friendly relationship
    C. obtain information about the kinds of people who come to the center
    D. convince the public that services are adequate

23. Officers should generally NOT use phrases like *too hard, too easy,* and *a lot* principally because such phrases

    A. may be offensive to some minority groups
    B. are too informal

C. mean different things to different people
D. are difficult to remember

24. The ability to communicate clearly and concisely is an important element in effective leadership.
Which of the following statements about oral and written communication is GENERALLY true?

   A. Oral communication is more time-consuming.
   B. Written communication is more likely to be misinterpreted.
   C. Oral communication is useful only in emergencies.
   D. Written communication is useful mainly when giving information to fewer than twenty people.

25. Rumors can often have harmful and disruptive effects on an organization.
Which one of the following is the BEST way to prevent rumors from becoming a problem?

   A. Refuse to act on rumors, thereby making them less believable
   B. Increase the amount of information passed along by the *grapevine*
   C. Distribute as much factual information as possible
   D. Provide training in report writing

KEY (CORRECT ANSWERS)

1. C		11. C	
2. D		12. A	
3. B		13. A	
4. B		14. A	
5. A		15. C	
6. B		16. A	
7. B		17. A	
8. C		18. B	
9. A		19. C	
10. B		20. A	

21. D
22. A
23. C
24. B
25. C

EXAMINATION SECTION
TEST 1

DIRECTIONS: Each question or incomplete statement is followed by several suggested answers or completions. Select the one that BEST answers the question or completes the statement. *PRINT THE LETTER OF THE CORRECT ANSWER IN THE SPACE AT THE RIGHT.*

1. When training your subordinates in a new method of crowd control, which one of the following techniques SHOULD be used?

    A. Teach them the whole job at one time, whether it contains a great many steps or only a few
    B. Issue orders without giving reasons because this will result in more questions and delays
    C. Explain and demonstrate, one step at a time
    D. Use technical language in order to make instructions precise

2. It is sometimes necessary to provide additional training for staff members who are poor in their performance of specific tasks.
    Of the following, the MOST effective way of improving staff performance is to

    A. use visual aids along with reading material to train staff on the general subject involved
    B. train subordinates to perform only those tasks which they normally perform
    C. plan and carry out programs to meet the subordinates' real work needs
    D. provide training only for staff members performing critical tasks

3. Assume that as a superior officer you confront one of your subordinate officers with the fact that he is not performing his job effectively. The officer tries to avoid the blame and shifts the criticism to other officers including yourself.
    Which one of the following is NOT a good way of handling this situation?

    A. Speaking and acting in an impartial and fair-minded manner
    B. Trying to determine why the officer finds it difficult to accept justifiable criticism
    C. Calling in the other officers whom this subordinate has criticized and having them discuss the matter with him
    D. Listening to the officer, at least at the outset, rather than interrupting his statement

4. For a superior officer to discuss a subordinate's performance evaluation with him is GENERALLY

    A. *inadvisable;* such a discussion will discourage a good worker
    B. *advisable;* the subordinate must know about the quality of his performance for improvement to occur
    C. *inadvisable;* a good performance evaluation will result in the subordinate's asking for more responsibility
    D. *advisable;* such discussions generally lead to a change in the subordinate's evaluation

5. The one of the following which is the MAJOR cause of employee lateness is

   A. low morale
   B. excessive fatigue
   C. accidents
   D. sickness

6. For officers to work together smoothly, teamwork is necessary.
   Which one of the following statements BEST describes the relationship between leadership and teamwork?

   A. Leadership cannot exist without teamwork.
   B. Teamwork cannot exist without leadership.
   C. Leadership and teamwork are one and the same.
   D. There is no relationship between leadership and teamwork.

7. For superiors who wish to achieve proper discipline among subordinates, it is generally MOST difficult to

   A. obtain rapid compliance with orders and directives
   B. prevent subordinates from questioning orders that are issued to them
   C. achieve compliance with orders while encouraging individual initiative
   D. use punishment to prevent infractions of the rules

8. Of the following, it is MOST likely that laxity in administering discipline will result in

   A. a loss of respect for their superior on the part of subordinates
   B. the satisfactory completion of the organization's job
   C. an increase in the number of disturbances at centers
   D. the establishment of proper conditions for successful administration

9. In dealing with a subordinate who shows a lack of interest in performing his duties, a superior officer should GENERALLY

   A. assign to him all the difficult work
   B. give him more responsibility
   C. inspect his performance more often than usual
   D. give him direct, detailed orders

10. A superior officer who has a highly motivated group of officers under his command GENERALLY

    A. shows an interest in how they are doing and is willing to back them up
    B. spends most of his time in closely supervising his subordinates
    C. supervises mainly through one of his subordinate officers
    D. is management-oriented rather than subordinate-oriented

11. As a superior, you might have to supervise subordinate officers who are very enthusiastic and ambitious.
    Which one of the following is the BEST reason for carefully watching the work of such officers?
    They

    A. may produce so much work that other officers resent them
    B. may appear to be overly concerned about being promoted
    C. might make decisions before obtaining the necessary information
    D. may be seeking the superior's job

12. In dealing with the public, officers should behave with courtesy. 12.____
Which one of the following practices would be LEAST effective in promoting courtesy?

    A. Giving advice on subjects about which you are not well informed
    B. Learning to take constructive criticism intelligently
    C. Avoiding discussions of a personal nature
    D. Treating members of the public as you would like to be treated

13. When directing the officers under your command, which one of the following is generally 13.____
the MOST effective method of supervision?

    A. Provide your directions through written orders to prevent misunderstanding
    B. Supervise every detail of the work closely so that it is carried out exactly as you want it
    C. Limit your concern to getting the job done and not to the people doing the work
    D. Set up general standards and goals so that officers have leeway as to how to achieve them

14. Leadership is particularly important in the security field. 14.____
Of the following, people GENERALLY expect their leader to

    A. state, *Do as I say, not as I do*
    B. refuse to allow changes in orders
    C. get many of his ideas from his subordinates
    D. take his feelings out on those who make mistakes

15. The MOST important single factor in the selection of a person for assignment to a position of greater responsibility should be his 15.____

    A. demonstrated ability to do the job
    B. schooling, both civilian and military
    C. training and experience on the job
    D. length of service

16. Security training received by security officers and noted in their personnel charts or 16.____
records should NOT be used as a basis for

    A. indicating individual degrees of skill
    B. assigning officers to particular shifts
    C. establishing priorities of instruction
    D. presenting a consolidated picture of the training status

17. As a superior officer, you note that one of your subordinates has not been performing his 17.____
job properly. You discover that the cause of this problem seems to be that he drinks excessively when off duty.
Of the following, the BEST way to handle this situation is to

    A. discipline the officer to the fullest extent possible
    B. discuss the problem and possible solutions with the officer's fellow workers
    C. wait until the officer has straightened himself out and then counsel him
    D. have a blunt and firm talk with the officer and direct him to seek treatment

18. Officers who are overly sensitive to criticism are one of the problems that superiors must deal with.
Of the following, which is the BEST way to handle such officers?
They should

    A. not be talked to differently from other officers
    B. be criticized only on serious mistakes
    C. not be criticized at all
    D. be reassured of their worth to their unit

19. A superior officer who suspects an employee of petty office theft calls the employee to his office and questions him directly.
In this situation, the superior's action is

    A. *desirable,* primarily because the subordinate should be allowed to answer these accusations privately
    B. *desirable,* primarily because confrontation will persuade the employee to tell the truth
    C. *undesirable,* primarily because line department personnel should handle such matters
    D. *undesirable,* primarily because direct confrontation might unnecessarily embarrass the employee

20. Assume that a certain superior officer assigns a task, without explanation, to a new subordinate who is not yet accepted by the work group.
Of the following, the MOST likely result of this action would be to

    A. encourage the subordinate to perform at his best
    B. make the subordinate feel insecure about proving himself
    C. stimulate other officers to do their best to impress the new staff member
    D. cause the experienced officers to feel inferior

21. A newly appointed superior officer often faces the problem of supervising officers who were formerly close personal friends of his.
In this situation, the one of the following which is the BEST approach to take toward these officers is to

    A. break all ties with former friends
    B. stay personally close with friends as this is always an advantage on the job
    C. maintain a relationship of easy, occasional familiarity
    D. become businesslike on the job but remain close socially

22. Assume that you, as a superior officer, are talking over a proposed change in procedure with your subordinates which would require their full cooperation.
Which one of the following actions would be MOST appropriate for you to take if your subordinates suggest modifications in the procedure?

    A. Prepare arguments against your subordinates' suggestions while you are listening to them
    B. Refuse to accept suggestions for changes since procedures can't be modified
    C. Listen carefully since your subordinates' suggestions may have merit
    D. Accept the recommendations of your more experienced subordinates

23. The successful supervisor should be aware that two of his most important assets are patience and understanding.
Of the following actions by a supervisor, the one that is LEAST likely to demonstrate these qualities would be to

   A. make deadlines realistic and reachable
   B. reprimand an employee the minute he makes a mistake
   C. assist employees in work-related problems
   D. discuss changes in procedures with subordinates

24. One of a supervisor's goals should be to create and maintain a force of loyal subordinates with high morale. This objective is likely to be achieved by all of the following EXCEPT

   A. making subordinate officers feel that their job is an important one
   B. encouraging supervisors to be concerned with the individual needs of subordinates
   C. giving subordinate officers an opportunity to express their thoughts, likes, and interests to their supervisors
   D. having supervisors rely only on the advice of trusted employees when resolving disputes between subordinates

25. One of a supervisor's major responsibilities is to evaluate the performance of his subordinates.
Which one of the following practices would be LEAST productive in developing meaningful evaluations from performance interviews?

   A. Make positive statements only
   B. Outline the points to discuss
   C. Adjust to the individual and situation
   D. Allow the employee to participate

KEY (CORRECT ANSWERS)

1. C
2. C
3. C
4. B
5. A

6. B
7. C
8. A
9. B
10. A

11. C
12. A
13. D
14. C
15. A

16. B
17. D
18. D
19. A
20. B

21. C
22. C
23. B
24. D
25. A

TEST 2

DIRECTIONS: Each question or incomplete statement is followed by several suggested answers or completions. Select the one that BEST answers the question or completes the statement. *PRINT THE LETTER OF THE COREECT ANSWER IN THE SPACE AT THE RIGHT.*

1. Assume that you are a superior officer concerned with improving the attitude of your subordinates toward their work.
   Of the following, the action that is MOST likely to improve this attitude would be for you to

   A. allow your subordinates to take extra time off
   B. interpret rules and regulations leniently
   C. request a merit increase in salary for your subordinates
   D. train your subordinates to perform at the highest possible level

   1._____

2. Assume that two of the officers under your command are hotly disputing the accuracy of a log book entry. One of the officers asks for your opinion.
   Which of the following would be LEAST advisable for you to do in this situation?

   A. Ask the officers to present their views calmly
   B. Keep your temper and remain impartial
   C. Stop the argument and then give your decision
   D. Judge the argument in proportion to its importance

   2._____

3. A superior officer notices that one of his subordinates is not doing his job.
   In this situation, it would be MOST appropriate for the superior officer to

   A. caution the subordinate officer promptly
   B. ignore the incident this time
   C. check on the subordinate officer's behavior in an hour
   D. warn the subordinate officer at the end of his work day that a report may be filed

   3._____

4. A recently appointed superior officer finds it difficult to make the decisions required in his new position.
   Which one of the following suggestions would be MOST helpful to him in overcoming this problem?

   A. Don't be concerned because everyone makes mistakes, and any mistake caused by your decisions will be ignored.
   B. Remember that you will be judged by the long-range soundness of all of your decisions.
   C. Since you are now in charge of a number of officers, let them bear the decision-making responsibility.
   D. Remember that you have a superior and that he can make the decision for you.

   4._____

5. Of the following, the BEST reason for a superior officer to nake inspections and rounds is to

   A. observe the physical appearance of personnel
   B. determine whether communication equipment is working properly

   5._____

49

C. decide whether adequate records are being kept
D. see that the performance of subordinates conforms with departmental standards

6. Assume that you, as a superior officer, have made an inspection and have submitted recommendations for improvements.
Which one of the following actions should be taken to assure that the desired results are obtained from the inspection?
You should

   A. distribute copies of the recommendations to all members of the force
   B. follow-up to determine whether the recommended improvements have been made
   C. give credit to other officers when it is due in order to help increase morale
   D. set up a schedule so that you inspect once a week

7. Assume that you have noticed that one of your subordinates has been quiet and rather depressed for two to three days with no change in his usual satisfactory job performance.
Of the following, the BEST action for you to take in this situation is to

   A. ask him to describe his feelings in detail
   B. act as if you noticed no change in the subordinate's behavior
   C. tell him to forget what's bothering him
   D. recommend that he seek professional guidance

8. Assume that you wish to introduce a change in your subordinates' work procedures in order to improve their performance.
Of the following, the BEST way to gain acceptance of this change is for you to

   A. stress its positive aspects
   B. downgrade past practices
   C. delay discussing it for a while
   D. order your subordinates to follow the new procedure at once

9. Suppose you come across two of your subordinate officers having an argument about the boundaries of their patrol posts.
Which of the following is the LEAST advisable course of action for you to take after stopping the argument?

   A. Tell the officers to speak with you individually
   B. Have the officers submit their views in writing for you to evaluate properly when you have time
   C. Meet with both officers in your office after they finish their tours
   D. Tell the officers to consult you on such matters in the future

10. Assume that a superior officer is explaining a new rule to his men at roll call. One officer states that he does not like the rule. The superior tells the officer that he agrees with him, but that the rule must be followed anyway. In this situation, the superior officer's statement was

    A. *proper,* chiefly because the men should know where superiors stand on rules and regulations
    B. *improper,* chiefly because superiors should not indicate disagreement with a change in rules since they must enforce them

C. *proper,* chiefly because efficiency improves when supervisors and subordinates agree on new rules
D. *improper,* chiefly because questions regarding rule changes should be answered at staff meetings rather than at roll call

11. Assume that you find that several of your subordinate officers have not performed satisfactorily during the last few emergency situations at your work location. The one of the following actions which is LEAST likely to improve their performance is for you to

    A. keep the subordinates informed about how they performed after each emergency
    B. stay alert for officers who are having difficulty with their work
    C. circulate among the officers at emergencies
    D. avoid the use of criticism

11.____

12. Of the following qualifications for an officer, the one that is MOST important is the ability to

    A. understand and get along with people
    B. write a good report
    C. overcome resistance to arrest
    D. solve crimes

12.____

13. Assume that you have noticed that one of your subordinate officers makes errors when questioning clients. You discuss with him the proper method to use when questioning clients.
Of the following, your NEXT step should be to

    A. ask another officer to check on your subordinate's procedure when questioning clients
    B. tell the officer to discuss with others how they question clients
    C. have the officer report regularly to you about the clients he questions
    D. watch the officer to see how he questions clients

13.____

14. One of the MOST important rules to follow when communicating with your superior is:

    A. Report everything that happens at your work location to him
    B. Pass on to him rumors and gossip heard within your center
    C. Let him hear from you first about any unusual success, problem or error
    D. Assign to one of your subordinates the responsibility of communicating with your supervisor

14.____

15. A superior officer may be required to instruct subordinates in the performance of their tasks.
Which of the following would NOT be proper when instructing a small group of employees?

    A. Use simple language
    B. Explain the procedure and the reason for the procedure
    C. Demonstrate one step at a time
    D. Use the lecture method instead of the discussion method whenever possible

15.____

16. Assume that a new officer has joined your unit. Which of the following approaches should you, as his superior officer, use in introducing him to the job?

    A. Put him right to work; he will learn best through his mistakes
    B. Act sternly, thereby gaining his respect and indicating the proper supervisor-subordinate relationship
    C. Give him the overall picture of the department and unit he is in
    D. Praise him, even when he makes errors, in order to gain his confidence

17. When a new officer begins work, he will often perform tasks ineffectively, thus requiring corrective action by his supervisor.
    In this situation, which one of the following represents the MOST desirable course of action for the supervisor?

    A. Point out specific errors in performance and how to correct them
    B. Tell the new officer that he is not doing the job properly and assign him to a new task
    C. Avoid criticism in the beginning since it may result in bitterness
    D. Do not criticize because criticism is not currently considered an acceptable tool of management

18. Of the following types of work, the one that is MOST likely to lead to dissatisfaction is work that is

    A. difficult to perform   B. tiring to complete
    C. uncomplicated   D. unimportant

19. When instructing subordinates to perform new tasks, the one of the following that is LEAST important in helping then to learn is to

    A. explain the procedure to them in a step-by-step manner
    B. show them what they must do
    C. let them do the task under guidance
    D. have them perform the task without supervision so they may learn from their mistakes

20. Which one of the following is the MOST important single thing to bear in mind about giving orders?

    A. An order should be given to a capable employee, not an uncooperative one.
    B. If an order is given correctly, you will not have to check the work.
    C. An order should be given in as forceful a manner as possible to assure that it is understood.
    D. An order is given because it is necessary to bring about certain results.

21. Suppose that a subordinate asks you about a rumor he has heard. The rumor deals with a subject which your superiors consider *confidential*.
    Which of the following BEST describes how you should answer the officer?
    Tell

    A. the officer that you don't make the rules and that he should speak to higher ranking officers
    B. the officer that you will ask your superior for information

C. him only that you cannot comment on the matter
D. him the rumor is not true

22. Superior officers often find it difficult to *get their message across* when instructing newly appointed officers in their various duties.
The MAIN reason for this is generally that the

   A. duties of the officers have increased
   B. superior officer is often so expert in his area that he fails to see it from the learner's point of view
   C. superior officer adapts his instruction to the slowest learner in the group
   D. new officers are younger, less concerned with job security, and more interested in fringe benefits

23. Assume that you are discussing a security problem with an officer under your command. During the discussion, you see that the officer's eyes are turning away from you and that he is not paying attention.
In order to get the officer's attention, you should FIRST

   A. ask him to look you in the eye
   B. talk to him about sports
   C. tell him he is being very rude
   D. change your tone of voice

24. As a superior officer, you may find it necessary to conduct meetings with your subordinates.
Of the following, which would be MOST helpful in assuring that a meeting accomplishes the purpose for which it was called?

   A. Give notice of the conclusions you would like to reach at the start of the meeting
   B. Delay the start of the meeting until everyone is present
   C. Write down points to be discussed in proper sequence
   D. Make sure everyone is clear on whatever conclusions have been reached and on what must be done after the meeting

25. Every superior officer will occasionally be called upon to deliver a reprimand to a subordinate. If done properly, this can greatly help an officer improve his performance.
Which one of the following is NOT a good practice to follow when giving a reprimand?

   A. Maintain your composure and temper
   B. Reprimand a subordinate in the presence of other officers so they can learn the same lesson
   C. Try to understand why the officer was not able to perform satisfactorily
   D. Let your knowledge of the officer involved determine the exact nature of the reprimand

KEY (CORRECT ANSWERS)

1. D
2. C
3. A
4. B
5. D

6. B
7. B
8. A
9. B
10. B

11. D
12. A
13. D
14. C
15. D

16. C
17. A
18. D
19. D
20. D

21. B
22. B
23. D
24. D
25. B

TEST 3

DIRECTIONS: Each question or incomplete statement is followed by several suggested answers or completions. Select the one that BEST answers the question or completes the statement. *PRINT THE LETTER OF THE CORRECT ANSWER IN THE SPACE AT THE RIGHT.*

1. Of the following, the PRIMARY purpose of communications between subordinates and superiors is to

    A. develop language skills
    B. enable subordinates to air their grievances
    C. help establish friendly ties
    D. solve job problems

2. Of the following, the MOST necessary elements of good communication are

    A. openness and form
    B. details and subjectivity
    C. speed and dependability
    D. length and appearance

3. Of the following, the MOST important role of a supervisor is that of

    A. being able to understand how his men feel about their assignments
    B. establishing good contacts with the administration
    C. fulfilling his responsibility to the assigned position
    D. presenting a good public image on the behalf of his organization

4. Of the following, the LEAST desirable behavior of a senior officer would be for him to

    A. attempt to gain the respect of superiors
    B. attempt to find causes of high employee turnover
    C. ignore infrequent latenesses
    D. ignore suggestions which may prove unworthy

5. A senior officer who consults with his subordinates about operational planning is GENERALLY

    A. attempting to prove his supervisory ability
    B. developing their job participation and cooperation
    C. passing down his responsibilities to others
    D. searching for an employee with supervisory ability

6. If a senior officer conducted supervision and inspection programs in order to become aware of his men's conduct, he would GENERALLY be considered to be

    A. excessively strict and authoritarian
    B. looking for potential troublemakers
    C. overconscientious in his work
    D. performing a vital duty

7. Of the following, the BEST reason for a supervisor's evaluation of his own on-the-job performance is to enable him to

    A. find the best methods of supervising his men and in getting the job done
    B. give the impression that he is sincere in trying to become a better supervisor

C. make a favorable impression on his superiors
D. make his work seem more important than it actually is

8. Assume that you are a senior officer making a performance evaluation of an officer. The reason for NOT drawing conclusions too quickly is CHIEFLY that

   A. without due consideration of all the facts, you are likely to evaluate the officer on biased personal judgment
   B. evaluation reports take a great deal of time and thought
   C. senior officers must consult with superiors before drawing conclusions about a subordinate's performance
   D. the officer might try to disprove any wrong information which you may have obtained about him

9. A senior officer notices two officers, known to be good workers, playing practical jokes and pranks on the other employees.
   In this case, disciplinary action is

   A. *desirable,* chiefly because horseplay on the job is not, strictly speaking, against the rules
   B. *undesirable,* chiefly because good workers tend to correct their own improper actions
   C. *desirable,* chiefly because horseplay could provoke other employees and that would disrupt normal work routine
   D. *undesirable,* chiefly because a supervisor should not get involved with employees' affairs

10. Resistance to or resentment of training is likely to be an attitude shown by many officers. Therefore, it is important for a senior officer to understand the causes of his men's attitudes and learn how to deal with them. Of the following, which is the BEST method of lessening an officer's resentment of training?

    A. Give the officers extra time off for taking part in the training program
    B. Openly criticize the officer who often makes mistakes during training
    C. Recommend promotions for those who complete the training program quickest
    D. Explain that the purpose of the training is to help them perform their jobs more efficiently

11. A senior officer required all officers under his supervision to submit a weekly report based on information from their daily log (memo) entries. The senior officer did not examine these reports, but he did file them as proof that the officers were not *sleeping* on the job.
    In general, this practice of the senior officer is considered

    A. *correct,* chiefly because the senior officer has little need of the reports since he is usually on the scene to observe the performance of his men
    B. *incorrect,* chiefly because, if the senior officer asked for reports, he should read or use the information they contain
    C. *correct,* chiefly because any information an officer had could only be based on daily occurrences
    D. *incorrect,* chiefly because the senior officer is placing too much emphasis on accuracy of paper work

12. Selecting an employee to be trained for performing the supervisor's duties is generally considered

    A. *desirable*, chiefly because it allows the supervisor to avoid many of his duties
    B. *undesirable*, chiefly because it creates the impression that the supervisor is showing favoritism
    C. *desirable*, chiefly because supervisory coverage is assured in the absence of the supervisor
    D. *undesirable*, chiefly because the trainee will cause the supervisor to worry about possible competition and thus neglect the performance of his duties

13. When discussing lateness with an employee, a supervisor should take the employee to an area where the problem can be discussed privately
    Generally, this practice is considered

    A. *desirable*, chiefly because it gives the employee an opportunity to converse with the supervisor in a very casual way
    B. *desirable*, chiefly because it keeps the problem from being discussed in front of an audience
    C. *undesirable*, chiefly because isolating an employee from his co-workers causes the *rumor-mongers* to spread false gossip about the matter
    D. *undesirable*, chiefly because trivial matters can be mentioned in the open without any repercussions

14. When an officer shows a pattern of abuse in his use of sick leave, a senior officer should

    A. ask the officer for medical proof of all future illnesses
    B. discourage other officers from abusing sick leave by giving the offending officer a public warning
    C. interview the officer and inquire about the reasons for his behavior
    D. acknowledge the officer's right to sick leave as set forth in departmental rules and regulations

15. Of the following, the MAJOR reason why grapevines generally develop in an agency is that

    A. employees have too much idle time
    B. employees want to socialize and gossip with other employees while working
    C. superior officers avoid reporting bad news downward from management to subordinates
    D. there is a communication gap between management and employees

16. If a newly-assigned senior officer is doubtful about the exact details of the assignment he is about to give to an officer, he should GENERALLY

    A. ask to speak to the officer in private and give him another assignment
    B. delay giving the assignment until he clears up his own doubt
    C. attempt to explain to the officer what he knows about the assignment in the best possible way
    D. put the assignment in writing

17. Of the following situations, which one would justify a supervisor's giving direct orders to another supervisor's subordinate?

   A. A supervisor away from his normal assignment observes a serious disturbance and gives orders to the officers in that area.
   B. A supervisor foresees a problem that will arise the next day in another district and immediately proceeds to inform the other supervisor's officers of the action they should take.
   C. A supervisor tells an officer under another supervisor to perform a duty a week from today because he feels it is an urgent matter.
   D. None of the above situations would justify direct supervision by any senior officer.

18. In the planning process, which of the following is NOT a recommended practice in preparing your final plan of action?

   A. Obtain all important available facts related to the problem
   B. Clarify the problem before any plan is created
   C. Make the plan easy to understand so that it can be carried out efficiently
   D. Never make assumptions or forecasts about what could occur

19. Of the following, the BEST way for a senior officer to get his subordinates to carry out his orders is to

   A. explain whenever possible why the orders are being given
   B. let subordinates know in advance the penalties for disobeying his orders
   C. describe the steps that must be followed in performing each order
   D. issue all orders in the form of direct and positive commands

20. It is MOST correct to state that race prejudice is to the GREATEST extent

   A. an inborn human characteristic
   B. the result of training and group association
   C. the product of ghetto areas
   D. a condition limited to adults only

21. *Scapegoating* is a form of prejudice which results MAINLY from

   A. degrading minority groups in an effort to secure status for one's own group
   B. shifting the blame for social inadequacies and ills from oneself to others
   C. thinking of people not as individual persons but rather placing them in carelessly formed, all-embracing classifications
   D. maintaining the existing order to prevent other groups from rising in social and economic status

22. The MOST important step in democratic supervision is

   A. allowing the employee a chance to apologize whenever he makes an error
   B. keeping tight control over employees
   C. making the employee realize that he needs your approval in order to keep his position
   D. showing an interest in the welfare of the employee

23. Evaluating a subordinate's likes and dislikes concerning his work is GENERALLY considered to be   23._____

    A. valuable in assigning work details to the subordinate
    B. necessary only when the subordinate complains of dissatisfaction with his daily duties
    C. unnecessary and a waste of time
    D. useful only in establishing a good relationship with the subordinate

24. Employee motivation is very critical in keeping up the morale of employees.   24._____
    Of the following, which is generally the BEST method of supervision which both motivates and maintains high morale?

    A. Aid employees in finding satisfaction in their assignments even if it requires extra time and responsibility
    B. Allow employees to work with a free hand and without daily interruptions
    C. Don't get involved or become concerned with interests or problems of employees outside the job
    D. Prove your friendship to a select number of employees so that the remainder of the staff will feel you are a *good guy* to work for

25. When attempting to motivate an experienced individual, it is BEST for a senior officer to appeal to the person's   25._____

    A. emotions
    B. positive interests
    C. negative feelings
    D. inhibitions

KEY (CORRECT ANSWERS)

1. D		11. B	
2. C		12. C	
3. C		13. B	
4. D		14. C	
5. B		15. D	
6. D		16. B	
7. A		17. A	
8. A		18. D	
9. C		19. A	
10. D		20. B	

21. B
22. D
23. A
24. A
25. B

EXAMINATION SECTION
TEST 1

DIRECTIONS: Each question or incomplete statement is followed by several suggested answers or completions. Select the one that BEST answers the question or completes the statement. *PRINT THE LETTER OF THE CORRECT ANSWER IN THE SPACE AT THE RIGHT.*

1. One of the basic characteristics of a good police supervisor is the courage to accept his supervisory responsibilities and to avoid making excuses and explanations. Of the following, the MOST valid deduction to make from this statement is that the supervisor should

   A. hold subordinates strictly to account so that he is not unjustly blamed
   B. not be required to assume responsibility for the error of a subordinate
   C. not seek to evade blame by referring to the inadequacies of his subordinates
   D. not accept excuses or explanations from his subordinates if they do not perform their duties properly

   1.____

2. A rather complex change is to be made in patrol procedures. As a supervising officer, it is your responsibility to make sure that your subordinates are informed of this change. The one of the following courses of action which is MOST likely to result in good performance is for you to

   A. assign one of your best officers to explain the order
   B. distribute an exact copy of the new order as soon as it becomes available
   C. explain the new procedure after your subordinates have had some experience with it
   D. explain the new procedure carefully before it is adopted

   2.____

3. As a supervising police officer, you have noticed that, upon the issuance of verbal orders by you to officers, there are seldom any questions asked by them seeking clarification of such orders. You have also noticed that, upon questioning the officers while on patrol, few of them have really understood your orders.
   Of the following courses of action, the one which constitutes the BEST solution to this problem is for you to

   A. question the officers immediately following the issuance of your orders
   B. take disciplinary action against those who are not able to understand your orders
   C. issue your orders in written form so that they may be understood more readily
   D. request that your commanding officer issue the orders

   3.____

4. A certain officer has a habit of issuing orders and giving directions to other officers on his own responsibility without having received the permission of the supervising officer to do so. Sometimes this occurs in the presence of the supervising officer whose silence on these occasions is interpreted as approval.
   This practice is

   A. *bad;* it must result in poorer performance by the other officers
   B. *good;* it helps develop leadership qualities in particular officers who indicate a willingness to accept responsibility

   4.____

61

C. *bad;* it creates an uncertainty in the minds of the other officers about whether a particular order should be obeyed
D. *good;* it makes the work of the supervising officer easier

5. As a supervising police officer, you have observed in your subordinates a consistent lack of attention to several minor patrol duties.
The BEST of the following actions for you to take FIRST is to

   A. attempt to perform these minor duties yourself
   B. take no action on the situation unless this lack of attention spreads to important duties
   C. instruct your subordinates concerning the necessity for performing all duties
   D. request the Chief to speak to your subordinates concerning the situation

6. As a supervising police officer, you have directed a subordinate to follow a specific route while on patrol. You later discover the subordinate patrolling an area outside the designated route.
The one of the following which is the BEST course of action for you to take FIRST is to

   A. explain to the subordinate your reasons for assigning him to the designated route
   B. question the subordinate concerning his reason for not following the designated route
   C. send him back to the designated route immediately
   D. take disciplinary action against the subordinate

7. A newly appointed supervising police officer has decided that he will give equal supervisory attention to each of his subordinates. Such a decision by this supervising officer is

   A. *wise;* all of the subordinates are thereby assured of fair and impartial treatment
   B. *unwise;* the amount of supervisory attention should be varied according to the needs of individual subordinates
   C. *wise;* such a decision will permit the supervising officer to devote more of time to actual patrol
   D. *unwise;* such a decision should be postponed until the Chief can be consulted

8. The one of the following which does NOT constitute an acceptable purpose of the disciplinary process in a police organization is to

   A. improve and maintain the morale of the department
   B. improve the individual whose work falls below defined standards of job performance
   C. provide a strict system of equal punishments for similar offenses
   D. raise or maintain the prestige of the department in the community

9. One of the officers under your supervision has suddenly become very careless in his personal appearance, and his job performance has fallen below the required standard. Questioning of the officer reveals that this condition is due to a serious personal problem. For you to assist in the solving of this problem is

   A. *improper;* your police background and training make it unlikely that you could provide any real assistance
   B. *proper;* all personal problems of your officers should be your concern

C. *improper;* you would be intruding upon the officer's right to privacy in personal matters
D. *proper;* the officer's personal problem has seriously affected his work

10. A community resident has asked an officer to recommend a good television repairman. For the officer to make such a recommendation would be

   A. *proper;* the officer is performing a service that will help a community resident
   B. *improper;* the officer is not qualified to know a good television repairman from a poor one
   C. *proper;* the officer can thus prevent the community resident from being victimized
   D. *improper;* the officer would be doing something that might affect his effectiveness as a law enforcement officer

10._____

11. It is a generally accepted principle of supervision that disciplinary action should be taken quickly when it needs to be taken.
The one of the following statements which BEST supports the taking of prompt disciplinary action is that

   A. the accuracy of official disciplinary records will thereby be insured
   B. the offender is more likely to feel that the disciplinary action will be severe
   C. the supervisor is more likely to remember the details surrounding the offender's breach of discipline
   D. there is an avoidance of the prolonged aggravation caused by later disposition of the case

11._____

12. A supervising police officer has been informed by a certain officer under his supervision that he will soon resign his job and accept employment elsewhere.
In this situation, the BEST course of action for the supervising officer is to

   A. assign him to the most difficult tasks and tours in order to favor the men remaining
   B. avoid giving him new types of assignments
   C. find out what his new job is and then try to persuade him to remain
   D. refrain from assigning him to work involving any responsibility

12._____

13. Officer X has complained to you that Officer Y generally is favored by getting the more desirable assignments. For you, as a supervising police officer, to attempt to explain to Officer X the reason for these assignments of Officer Y would be

   A. *proper;* it is likely to lessen Officer X's objection
   B. *improper;* your authority as a supervisor would be weakened
   C. *proper;* it is needed in order to protect Officer Y from Officer X's resentment and jealousy
   D. *improper;* as a supervisor, there is no need for you to explain the assignments which you make

13._____

14. A community resident has complained to the supervising police officer that a certain officer makes a habit of asking him and other residents to buy tickets for dances. An investigation reveals that this is, so.
Of the following, the BEST course of action for the supervising officer is to

   A. advise the resident that he is under no obligation to buy any such tickets
   B. forbid the officer to sell these tickets, briefly explaining why

14._____

C. permit the sale of these tickets only if other groups are allowed equal opportunity to sell tickets to their affairs
D. tell the officer to use discretion in asking people to buy tickets and to avoid asking those who might complain

15. An officer has reprimanded a young boy for playing on the grass in a project. The boy's mother tells the officer that he should be more concerned with arresting criminals than with reprimanding children for petty violations.
Of the following, the BEST answer for the officer to make to this woman is that

   A. children must be taught good conduct by all those concerned for their welfare
   B. damage to public property means higher rents and higher taxes
   C. serious criminals often begin their careers with minor violations
   D. the police force does its best to enforce all laws and regulations

16. In view of the fact that police patrol activity is not able to eliminate all opportunities for criminal behavior, the one of the following procedures which is generally regarded as MOST desirable is for the patrol force to

   A. assign the entire available patrol force to those areas which have the greatest incidence of crime
   B. attempt to give an impression of omnipresence at every hour and in all sections of the community
   C. devote its major efforts to the creation of wholesome influences in a community
   D. keep a substantial patrol force in reserve to answer specific complaints received from the public

17. Although the system of three eight-hour shifts is generally employed by police departments, it would be MORE suitable to provide for overlapping shifts when

   A. an average work load for one shift is substantially less than the other shifts
   B. an hourly work load on one shift fluctuates widely from the average of the shift
   C. the average work load for one shift is substantially greater than the other shifts
   D. the hourly work loads in each of the shifts is almost the same as the average of that shift

18. The highest quality of patrol service results from the permanent assignment of an officer to the same post. The one of the following statements which is the LEAST important advantage of such permanent assignment is that under this system,

   A. it is more likely that events which do not fit into the normal pattern of activity on the post will be noticed
   B. the officer becomes well-acquainted with many persons residing on his post
   C. there is a saving of time and effort due to the familiarity of the officer with his post-relieving point
   D. there is less joint responsibility for conditions on any given post

19. The performance of continuous routine patrol service should generally be provided by the patrol division and not by special divisions.
This statement is

A. *true;* the patrol division should not be subordinated to any other police unit
B. *false;* special divisions frequently are staffed with many of the most competent housing officers
C. *true;* officers engaged in special patrol are less likely to be alert for patrol conditions outside the field of their specialization
D. *false;* special divisions have a basic patrol responsibility equal to that of the patrol division

20. Specialization in the performance of administrative planning duties is not an example of an undesirable specialization of duty being made at the expense of the patrol force.
This statement is GENERALLY

    A. *false;* specialization of any kind inevitably results in some depletion of the patrol force
    B. *true;* specialization is desirable to the extent that it efficiently performs part of the actual patrol duty
    C. *false;* this type of duty can be performed efficiently by the individual supervising officer
    D. *true;* these duties cannot be performed by officers in the course of their regular patrol

21. The one of the following which MOST indicates a definite need for the establishment of a specialized enforcement unit, in addition to the regular patrol force, is that

    A. a community group requests that extra enforcement activity be directed towards problems of public morals
    B. a substantial number of patrol personnel have been trained in specialized areas of police work
    C. business interests in the community demand police protection during transfers of cash to banks
    D. the patrol force is unable to perform the total police task in some area

22. The one of the following which indicates the BEST method by which a supervising police officer may check on the quality of patrol performance by the officers under his supervision is to

    A. ask the community residents if they are receiving satisfactory police service
    B. determine the number of arrests for serious crimes made by each officer
    C. observe the officers while they are actually performing patrol
    D. question the more experienced officers concerning the performance of other members of the force

23. The police force should de-emphasize the pursuit of criminals and stress crime prevention.
For a supervising police officer, this should mean that his CHIEF emphasis should be on the

    A. importance of complete patrol coverage
    B. importance of physical fitness
    C. proficiency of his subordinates with firearms
    D. value of morale in police work

24. Supervising police officers should be instructed how to use manpower to prevent distribution of forces on unproductive assignments.
This statement is

   A. *false;* only time can tell whether any assignment will be unproductive or not
   B. *true;* the supervising officer cannot perform any supervisory duty without such instructions
   C. *false;* assignments should be made solely in response to public demand for police protection
   D. *true;* the assignment of men should be aimed at securing the maximum police protection

25. An officer on patrol is approached by a resident who excitedly informs him that she has just observed a stranger trying the doors of several apartments on the second floor of the project building in which she lives. She also states that the stranger is wearing a dark hat and topcoat. The officer goes to the building and encounters a man hurriedly leaving, who is wearing a gray hat and topcoat. The officer questions him about his presence in the building. The action of the officer was

   A. *poor;* his duty is to go to the second floor as quickly as possible
   B. *good;* everyone in the vicinity of a crime who acts suspiciously should be arrested
   C. *poor;* the tenant stated that the stranger trying the doors was wearing a dark hat and topcoat
   D. *good;* the man about to leave the building may be the same one who was trying the apartment doors

KEY (CORRECT ANSWERS)

1.	C	11.	D
2.	D	12.	B
3.	A	13.	A
4.	C	14.	B
5.	C	15.	D
6.	B	16.	B
7.	B	17.	B
8.	C	18.	C
9.	D	19.	C
10.	D	20.	D

21. D
22. C
23. A
24. D
25. D

TEST 2

DIRECTIONS: Each question or incomplete statement is followed by several suggested answers or completions. Select the one that BEST answers the question or completes the statement. *PRINT THE LETTER OF THE CORRECT ANSWER IN THE SPACE AT THE RIGHT.*

1. A supervisor who is training several inexperienced subordinates on patrol in the best way to handle the various patrol situations likely to arise should respond with them to calls for their services and

    A. avoid correcting any mistakes as they are made to discuss the overall handling of the situation later
    B. correct all mistakes as they are made and also discuss the overall handling of the situation later
    C. correct all mistakes as they are made and then avoid future discussion of these mistakes
    D. correct serious mistakes as they are made and discuss the overall handling of the situation later

2. For an officer who is supervising patrol to make a notation in his memorandum book whenever he strongly reprimands a subordinate verbally is

    A. *inadvisable,* chiefly because an undue amount of supervisory time will be devoted to recording such information
    B. *advisable,* chiefly because the sergeant is developing a fund of information which will be useful in the future handling of the subordinate
    C. *inadvisable,* chiefly because the subordinate may resent such a procedure
    D. *advisable,* chiefly because all subordinates will make greater efforts to improve their job performance since they will not be sure of the nature of the notations

3. A supervisor is attempting to discuss some important and practical applications of a new law to police work with a group of his subordinates who have little knowledge of this law. He notices that the group is passive and uninterested in the discussion.
Of the following, it would be BEST for the supervisor to

    A. explain the law and its application carefully and as thoroughly as possible and ask provocative questions
    B. order the group to participate in the discussion since it is for their own good
    C. give the factual information on the law and then stay out of the discussion as much as possible
    D. postpone further discussion until some future time when the group has shown some interest in the law

4. While on patrol, a supervisor is required to issue a fairly important order to a subordinate. Due to the pressure of other duties, the supervisor issues the order very quickly and briefly while *on the run.*
An IMPORTANT weakness of the issuance of the order in this manner is that

    A. the subordinate is likely to regard the order as less important than it really is
    B. the supervisor is giving the subordinate more responsibility than is proper
    C. orders require explanation in order to convey the intended meaning
    D. the supervisor is likely to forget this order and to whom it was issued

5. In giving orders, a supervisor will give more details at certain times than at other times. The one of the following situations in which the LEAST amount of detail should be given is when the order is concerned with a procedure which

   A. has hazardous features
   B. is of a special or infrequent nature
   C. has been generally performed in a standardized manner
   D. is to be carried out by several subordinates of limited experience

6. Briefing a subordinate on the circumstances which have made an order necessary is desirable MAINLY because the

   A. subordinate thereby has greater respect for the supervisor for his demonstrated knowledge of the job
   B. supervisor is thereby making allowances for differences among subordinates in their ability to understand orders
   C. subordinate will not tend to view the order as a personal or arbitrary command
   D. supervisor will be better able to test the quality of the execution of the order by *follow-up* procedures

7. Disciplinary action will, in most instances, be initiated by the immediate superior of the person to be disciplined. This is so MAINLY because

   A. it permits the higher superiors to be able to devote most of their attention and effort to broader and more generalized problems of administration
   B. it helps to develop a forceful image of the immediate superior which will serve to prevent other overt acts of misconduct by other subordinates
   C. the immediate superior is the one most qualified to make recommendations as to the severity of punishment to be applied
   D. the immediate superior is usually in the best position to observe derelictions of duty requiring some kind of corrective action

8. Having decided to institute disciplinary action against a subordinate in his command, a supervisor speaks to the subordinate for the purpose of informing him of the action to be taken.
   At this interview, it would be LEAST advisable for the supervisor to explain to the subordinate

   A. the procedural steps which will follow the institution of disciplinary action
   B. the specific reason for the disciplinary action
   C. that the purpose of discipline is the punishment of the offender
   D. what is expected of the subordinate in the future, especially as related to the behavior which resulted in disciplinary action being taken

9. The repeated use by a superior officer of a call for volunteers to get a job done is objectionable MAINLY because

   A. it may create a feeling of animosity between the volunteers and the non-volunteers
   B. it may indicate that the superior is avoiding responsibility for making assignments which will be most productive
   C. it is an indication that the superior is not familiar with the individual capabilities of his men
   D. it is unfair to men who, for valid reasons, do not or cannot volunteer

10. Of the following statements concerning subordinates, expressions to a supervisor of their opinions and feelings concerning work situations, the one which is MOST correct is that

10.____

   A. by listening and responding to such expressions the supervisor encourages the development of complaints
   B. the lack of such expressions should indicate to the supervisor that there is a high level of job satisfaction
   C. the more the supervisor listens to and responds to such expressions, the more he demonstrates lack of supervisory ability
   D. by listening and responding to such expressions, the supervisor will enable many subordinates to understand and solve their own problems on the job

11. Usually one thinks of communication as a single step, essentially that of transmitting an idea. Actually, however, this is only part of a total process, the FIRST step of which should be

11.____

   A. the prompt dissemination of the idea to those who may be affected by it
   B. motivating those affected to take the required action
   C. clarifying the idea in one's own mind
   D. deciding to whom the idea is to be communicated

12. Research studies on patterns of informal communication have concluded that most individuals in a group tend to be passive recipients of news, while a few make it their business to spread it around in an organization.
With this conclusion in mind, it would be MOST correct for the supervisor to attempt to identify these few individuals and

12.____

   A. give them the complete facts on important matters in advance of others
   B. inform the other subordinates of the identity of these few individuals so that their influence may be minimized
   C. keep them straight on the facts on important matters
   D. warn them to cease passing along any information to others

13. The one of the following which is the PRINCIPAL advantage of making an oral report is that it

13.____

   A. affords an immediate opportunity for two-way communication between the subordinate and superior
   B. is an easy method for the superior to use in transmitting information to others of equal rank
   C. saves the time of all concerned
   D. permits more precise pinpointing of praise or blame by means of follow-up questions by the superior

14. Supervisory training is designed to develop skills in human relationships while work-skill training attempts to alter the relationship between a person and a machine or material of some sort.
The one of the following which MOST accurately describes an important difference between these two types of training is that

14.____

A. resistance to work-skill training is likely to be greater than resistance to supervisory training
B. skills acquired from supervisory training should be less flexible than skills acquired from work-skill training
C. skills acquired from supervisory training are usually less directly and routinely applied than skills acquired from work-skill training
D. trainees are more apt to feel more secure in attempting to utilize skills acquired through supervisory training than those acquired from work-skill training

15. The quantity and quality of work performed by one subordinate is below the level that he is capable of attaining. Because of this, the supervisor gives this subordinate the least difficult assignments only.
This action taken by the supervisor is

   A. *poor,* chiefly because the subordinate should be motivated to perform work of greater responsibility
   B. *good,* chiefly because each subordinate should be allowed to work in the manner he finds most satisfactory
   C. *poor,* chiefly because the supervisor should make his assignments such that all subordinates are given an equal amount of work and responsibility
   D. *good,* chiefly because otherwise the supervisor will have to give a greater amount of supervisory attention to this subordinate than to other subordinates

16. It has been the practice in some communities to substantially base the efficiency rating of police commanders on incidence of crime.
This practice is inadvisable MAINLY because

   A. crime figures also reflect many community factors beyond the control of the commander
   B. such figures may be incomplete and unreliable
   C. there is little or no relation between such figures and police efficiency
   D. there is a great need for improved techniques of processing and analysis of crime figures

17. Even though officers are assigned on a permanent basis to tours of duty at night, experts in plant security recommend that arrangements be made for them to make a complete tour of the premises during the daytime.
The CHIEF reason for this suggestion is to

   A. enable them to coordinate their patrol work better with that of the officers assigned to daytime duty
   B. discover those areas in which teenage groups congregate during the day and which are, therefore, most vulnerable to night-time crime
   C. allow them to become more familiar with the general layout of the premises and with specific locations that may be of importance to them in their work
   D. give them a clearer daytime view of the exact conditions they may expect to encounter during their tours of duty at night

18. It has been suggested that housing officers on duty at night record the names of all Authority employees remaining in or leaving the project considerably after their normal working hours.
The CHIEF reason for taking this precaution would be to

A. assist the housing police force in interrogating the supervisors of these employees to determine whether they have any valid reason for remaining after their working hours
B. enable the housing police force to determine more promptly whether these employees are involved in any illegal activity during their off-duty hours
C. assist the housing police force to direct its questioning to these employees if it later develops that something improper occurred during this period of time
D. enable the housing police force to scrutinize more closely the activities of these employees during their regular working hours

19. The one of the following which is a distinct advantage of an organization's special police force over the regular police force is that the special police force GENERALLY

    A. has a limited area of jurisdiction in which only certain types of crimes occur
    B. has a limited responsibility for exercising diligence in patrol
    C. is able to limit its surveillance to only those persons who are not tenants or employees
    D. knows that most persons with whom it comes in contact on post are known to it as tenants or employees of the organization

20. From a management point of view, the BEST of the following reasons why it is better for police to emphasize the prevention of theft and vandalism, rather than the detection of such crimes or the apprehension of persons involved, is that preventive measures generally

    A. expedite the more prompt reporting of acts of vandalism and thefts because any actual occurrence of such offenses would be made more obvious
    B. minimize the need for the more unpleasant and costly procedures involved in apprehending and prosecuting guilty employees
    C. result in offenders being easily caught in the act of committing the crime
    D. involve stricter screening of employees and thus prevent any would-be criminals from becoming employees

21. It is generally recommended that the security division or special force of an organization be organized and trained in the measures needed to disperse or control a milling crowd and prevent it from turning into a rioting mob CHIEFLY in order to

    A. avoid the necessity of seeking outside assistance in quelling a purely local disturbance involving the organization
    B. quickly isolate and apprehend the leaders of the mob so that the police can take proper punitive action
    C. prevent injury or death to persons and damage to organization plant and equipment
    D. prevent the mob from spreading out into territory where the special police force has no jurisdiction

22. The CHIEF reason why the issuance of identification badges should be carefully controlled and why one should never be reissued with the same serial number as one which has been previously reported lost is to

A. insure against duplications of identification and establish a clear record of who is authorized to possess a particular badge
B. minimize the possibility of their being stolen or counterfeited by unauthorized persons
C. make sure that identification badges are returned
D. prevent unauthorized persons from mutilating or altering a validly issued identification badge

23. The rotation of officers has been recommended, in terms of both time and place of operation.
The CHIEF of the following reasons for applying this recommendation to experienced officers would be to

    A. enable them to gain more experience by exposing them to the different supervisory methods of various superior officers
    B. keep them alert by making them uncertain as to the varying degrees of diligence required by the different superior officers to whom they are assigned
    C. prevent them from becoming overly friendly with the residents and shopkeepers in the neighborhood
    D. make them more aware of problems existing in the various communities

24. Supervisors often feel that police recruits today do not accept direction as willingly as in the past.
The one of the following which is the MOST likely explanation for such a reaction by some recruits is the

    A. emphasis on individuality found in the home and in the school which tends to substitute tolerance and freedom for strict discipline
    B. increasingly complex nature of society which does not permit authoritarian concepts of discipline
    C. negative reaction to authority of men who have fulfilled a required military service obligation
    D. current notion that frequent direction by superiors constitutes undemocratic supervision

25. Police officers on patrol are constantly warned to be on the alert for suspicious persons, actions, and circumstances. With this in mind, a supervisor should emphasize the need for them to

    A. be cautious and suspicious when dealing officially with any civilian, regardless of the latter's overt actions or the circumstances surrounding his dealings with the police
    B. become thoroughly familiar with the usual on their posts so as to be better able to detect the unusual
    C. take aggressive police action immediately against any unusual person or condition detected on their posts, regardless of any other circumstances
    D. keep looking for the unusual persons, actions, and circumstances on their posts and pay less attention to the usual occurrences

KEY (CORRECT ANSWERS)

1. D
2. B
3. A
4. A
5. C

6. C
7. D
8. C
9. B
10. D

11. C
12. C
13. A
14. C
15. A

16. A
17. C
18. C
19. D
20. B

21. C
22. A
23. C
24. A
25. B

TEST 3

DIRECTIONS: Each question or incomplete statement is followed by several suggested answers or completions. Select the one that BEST answers the question or completes the statement. *PRINT THE LETTER OF THE CORRECT ANSWER IN THE SPACE AT THE RIGHT.*

1. The most competent leaders seldom have to resort to a display of authority. Of the following, the MOST important quality of this type of leader is that he

   A. is able to inspire subordinates to perform satisfactorily
   B. makes sure that his men know the point beyond which punitive action will be taken
   C. secures compliance with orders by formalized disciplinary procedures
   D. secures compliance with orders by implied threats of disciplinary action

   1.___

2. Demands for more police officers are frequently made by police administrators before they have first adopted methods that will assure a more effective use of the present forces.
   In view of this statement, the BEST of the following guides to the most effective utilization of police personnel is the

   A. analysis of reports, complaints, and statistics to indicate needed services
   B. demands of various community groups for special kinds of police protection
   C. fullest use of new scientific equipment in records management
   D. requests of commanders of specialized units who seek to increase the effectiveness of their units by the assignment of additional men

   2.___

3. An organization such as a police agency is not generally confronted by such unique problems as to make impossible the application of certain administrative principles that have been found applicable in other organizations.
   Of the following, the MOST valid deduction to make from this statement is that

   A. practices of other organizations reveal that police problems are not generally susceptible to solution by standardized management techniques
   B. questions of size are relevant in evaluating the applicability of common administrative principles
   C. some management guides can serve both police and non-police administrators equally well
   D. superficial familiarity with police organizations often leads to the application of invalid administrative techniques

   3.___

4. Formal police training programs should generally be conducted during the officers' off-duty time; otherwise, the public funds allotted to police services are not being properly used.
   This statement is GENERALLY

   A. *false;* close supervision during the actual performance of duties provides the only practical training technique
   B. *true;* the most effective training is usually conducted in an environment completely different from the one in which job performance takes place
   C. *true;* only those training activities which relate to the performance of extremely difficult duties should be conducted during on-duty time
   D. *false;* more effective performance of duties by the trainees will compensate for any on-duty time devoted to training

   4.___

5. The ultimate responsibility for police training lies with the top echelon of command, and the supervising police officer should not properly be held accountable for any part of this supervisory function.
   This statement is

   A. *true;* the supervising police officer should devote the major portion of his time to the performance of patrol
   B. *false;* the supervising police officer is in a key position to assist in training
   C. *true;* the duty of a supervising police officer to correct the improper patrol performance of subordinates cannot be classified as training
   D. *false;* the supervising police officer's primary responsibility is the training of subordinates

6. Periodic training of all police personnel, experienced officers as well as recruits, is a necessary requirement for effective police operations.
   This statement is GENERALLY

   A. *false;* methods of police operation are relatively stable and, therefore, additional training is unnecessary
   B. *true;* experienced personnel and recruits both require continued training at essentially the same level
   C. *false;* such training would undermine the morale of the experienced officers and seriously affect their job performance
   D. *true;* the original training may be forgotten or made obsolete by changing community conditions and improved methods

7. There is considerable merit to the idea that the police agency have only one telephone number listed in the telephone directory so that the general public, when seeking police assistance, will be required to contact a central complaint desk.
   The one of the following which is the MOST important advantage of this procedure is that

   A. direct public contact with the central complaint desk will insure that the most appropriate police action will be taken
   B. it makes less likely the possibility of a complaint being ignored or not investigated
   C. it makes unnecessary any future public contact with the local police unit
   D. it prevents any complaints from being registered in any local police unit

8. A system of complete decentralization of police records, with the line operating units maintaining their own records, constitutes the most advisable system.
   This statement is GENERALLY

   A. *false;* decentralization of record keeping tends to turn the line operating units into small and almost independent police organizations
   B. *true;* decentralization of record keeping fixes responsibility in a manner superior to the centralization of record keeping
   C. *false;* such complete decentralization of records would prevent any coordination of the line operating units
   D. *true;* police records should remain in the unit of their origin so that ready reference may be made to them

9. Much of the difficulty encountered in the process of administrative communication arises from a failure to realize that many words have varied, rather than a single, meaning. Accordingly, in issuing complex orders, it would be MOST important for the newly appointed supervising police officer to

    A. carefully check the meaning of difficult words in proposed orders
    B. issue written orders, rather than verbal orders, wherever possible
    C. review and discuss the orders with his subordinates
    D. revise the wording of all orders in order to clarify their meaning

10. As a supervising police officer, you have informed your subordinates that the Chief wants them to come to him directly at any suitable time to discuss problems, grievances, or suggestions for improvement of patrol performance. You have noticed, after a lapse of several months, that none of your subordinates have gone to the Chief for any of these purposes.
    The one of the following which is the LEAST likely explanation of this reluctance on the part of your subordinates is

    A. the natural reluctance of subordinates to freely express their ideas in the presence of higher authority
    B. that the subordinates may be reluctant to bypass your authority as their immediate supervisor
    C. the fear of being considered *troublemakers* by other superior officers in the department
    D. that good supervision has completely eliminated problems, grievances, and the need for suggestions

11. As a supervising police officer, you feel that a certain officer under your supervision is responsible for starting several unfounded rumors concerning police matters in the precinct.
    Of the following possible courses of action, the one which would be the MOST effective in dealing with the problem is to

    A. ignore the situation since none of the rumors contained any elements of truth
    B. provide sufficient facts about police matters in the precinct to establish a basis upon which rumors may be evaluated
    C. institute formal disciplinary action against the suspected officer
    D. speak to your subordinates, as a group, on the undesirable effects of spreading false information

12. Although the increasing complexity of police work strongly favors the specialist, experienced administrators are alert to the dangers in this tendency and strive to maintain flexible arrangements whenever specialized techniques threaten unity of action.
    Of the following, the MOST valid conclusion from this statement is that

    A. complexity of police work requires specialization to insure unity of action
    B. flexibility is needed to offset the occasional undesirable effects of specialization
    C. the role of the specialist in police work has become more important due to the influence of experienced administrators
    D. unity of action, although increased by specialization, can at the same time be inflexible because of police complexity

13. The quality of police service is more strongly influenced by the competence of the individual members of the force than by any other single factor.
The one of the following aspects of police administration which contributes LEAST to the development of such competence is the

    A. absence of morale-destroying influences
    B. promptness and certainty of disciplinary procedures
    C. existence of a suitable recruit training program
    D. survey of needed changes in organizational structure

14. Some law enforcement agencies do not wait for the legal disposition of an arrest case by the courts but close the arrest record when their custody of a prisoner ends. Such a procedure is GENERALLY considered to be

    A. *good;* strict impartiality by the police in the administration of criminal law requires that they be unaffected by either the conviction or acquittal of a prisoner
    B. *good;* the long delays frequently accompanying court procedure would unduly add to the work involved in the record keeping function
    C. *poor;* the legal disposition of a case should have some bearing on evaluating the work of the agency
    D. *poor;* court dispositions provide the only sure indication of the quality of the police investigative procedures

15. A maintenance man continually brings to the attention of a housing officer matters of a minor nature about building upkeep which are not the proper concern of the housing officer force. The housing officer has told the maintenance man that these problems are not a concern of the housing police personnel. However, the maintenance man continues to bring these matters to the attention of the housing officer. The housing officer tells his supervising officer about the situation.
Of the following, the BEST course of action for the supervising officer to take is to

    A. advise the housing officer to listen to the complaints of the maintenance man and then to ignore them
    B. ask the housing manager to take steps to change the conduct of the maintenance man
    C. have the housing officer transferred to another assignment so that he will not come in contact with the maintenance man
    D. suggest to the housing manager that the maintenance man be transferred since the latter is interfering with police duties

16. The one of the following factors which provides the BEST indication of the number of officers to be assigned to the inspection of store doors during the night hours is the

    A. average distance between the stores to be inspected
    B. number of complaints received from the owners of the stores to be inspected
    C. number of man-hours required to perform these inspections properly
    D. number of stores that are to be inspected

17. When properly performed, patrol plays a leading role in the accomplishment of the police purpose of crime prevention CHIEFLY by

    A. apprehending offenders and impressing them with the omnipotence of the police
    B. being the only form of police service that directly attempts to eliminate the opportunities for crime

C. gaining public support by the prompt investigation of offenses and recovery of stolen property
D. influencing public attitudes against crime in its routine daily associations with the public

18. The theory of police patrol which, if properly applied, should have the GREATEST deterrent effect on crime is that which favors patrolling

    A. all areas in such a manner as to make the police officers as unnoticeable as possible
    B. all areas in such a manner as to attract the maximum of attention to the police
    C. areas of high incidence of crime in an obvious manner and on a frequent and fixed schedule
    D. areas of low incidence of crime obviously and irregularly and areas of high incidence of crime on an irregular schedule and attracting a minimum of attention

18.___

19. It has been said that police patrol should aim at giving the impression of omnipresence at all times.
The one of the following which is the PRIMARY reason for this statement is that generally the

    A. planning for successful theft must be changed by the potential offender's expectation of apprehension
    B. potential thief's desire to steal is diminished by the presence of a uniformed officer
    C. potential thief's belief in the opportunity for successful theft is diminished by his expectation of apprehension
    D. potential thief's desire to steal is diminished by his expectation of apprehension

19.___

20. Whenever new tasks and duties are assigned to the police force, the question arises as to whether they should be assigned to the regular patrol force or to a specialized unit.
It would be MOST desirable in such a situation for the new tasks and duties to be so assigned as to give the

    A. regular patrol force all tasks and duties which it can perform as well as if done by specialists and which do not interfere with regular patrol duties
    B. specialized units all tasks and duties which they can perform as efficiently as the regular patrol force
    C. regular patrol force only those tasks and duties which are clearly in keeping with patrol duties and which are of a non-specialized nature
    D. specialized units all those tasks and duties which are of a specialized nature regardless of their relationship to regular patrol duties

20.___

21. An undesirable result of specialization in police work is the

    A. assignment to regular patrol officers of the primary responsibility for the enforcement of regulations in specialized areas of enforcement
    B. assignment of regular patrol officers to render many services to the specialized branches of service
    C. performance by patrol officers during the course of their regular patrol of tasks which can be performed by specialists at any other time
    D. performance by specialists of tasks that should be performed by patrol officers in the course of their regular patrol

21.___

22. There has been a marked trend during the past thirty years toward a greater public demand for extra services from the patrol force and also a trend toward increased specialization in police work.
The CHIEF drawback to both of these tendencies is the

   A. difficulty of choosing the members of the force to be assigned to both these tasks
   B. decrease in the number of members of the force available for assignment to patrol
   C. poorer technical knowledge of the patrol sergeant in his supervisory dealings with police specialists
   D. reduction in authority and prestige of the members of the force assigned to patrol duties in contrast to that of those assigned to special units

23. It is not enough for a police agency's services to be of a high quality; attention must also be given to the acceptability of these services to the general public. This statement is GENERALLY

   A. *false;* a superior quality of police service automatically wins public support
   B. *true;* the police cannot generally progress beyond the understanding and support of the public
   C. *false;* the acceptance by the public of police services determines their quality
   D. *true;* the police are generally unable to engage in any effective enforcement activity without public support

24. Final decisions regarding quality and extent of police services to be provided should rest with those politically responsible for the conduct of a city's affairs.
The PRINCIPAL reason for this point of view is that

   A. only those officials responsible for the overall conduct of city affairs have the authority to make such decisions
   B. city and state legislation determine the limits of the activities of the police
   C. these officials have the advantage of readily available technical advice and information from police officials
   D. the level of governmental services is, in the final analysis, dependent solely upon budgetary considerations

25. Of the following, the LEAST likely way in which a records system may serve a supervising police officer is in

   A. developing a sympathetic and cooperative public attitude toward the police
   B. improving the quality of supervision by permitting a check on the accomplishment of subordinates
   C. permitting a precise prediction of the exact crime incidence in specific categories for the following year
   D. helping to take the guesswork out of the distribution of the force

KEY (CORRECT ANSWERS)

1. A
2. A
3. C
4. D
5. B

6. D
7. B
8. A
9. C
10. D

11. B
12. B
13. D
14. C
15. B

16. C
17. B
18. B
19. C
20. A

21. D
22. B
23. B
24. A
25. A

REPORT WRITING

EXAMINATION SECTION

TEST 1

DIRECTIONS: Each question or incomplete statement is followed by several suggested answers or completions. Select the one that BEST answers the question or completes the statement. *PRINT THE LETTER OF THE CORRECT ANSWER IN THE SPACE AT THE RIGHT.*

Questions 1-10.

DIRECTIONS: Questions 1 through 10 are to be answered SOLELY on the basis of the following passage and Stolen Vehicle Report Form, which appears on the following page. The form contains 43 numbered boxes. Read the passage and look at the form before answering the questions.

Police Officers Walton and Wright, patrolling in their radio patrol car in the industrial area of the 29th Precinct, were dispatched to 523 Johnson Boulevard at 10:30 A.M. on October 30, 2020 by the Police Radio Dispatcher. The Dispatcher had received a telephone call from a Ms. Ann Graham at 10:28 A.M. that her friend's car was being stolen from in front of her house.

Officers Walton and Wright arrived at 523 Johnson Boulevard at 10:32 A.M. Ms. Graham was waiting outside and informed them that the car had already been stolen. She stated that her friend, Samantha Merlin, had gone on vacation to California three days before and had left her car in Ms. Graham's care. Ms. Graham had parked the car in front of her own house the night before.

Ms. Graham stated that she looked out of her window at 10:25 A.M. that day and saw a strange man breaking into the car using a wire coat hanger. The car's hood was raised. She ran to her telephone to call the police. When she returned to her window, she saw the man doing something under the hood and, within a minute, he drove the car away. She had been too frightened to try to stop him, and there was no one else on the street.

Ms. Graham described the car as a black 2002 Buick 2-door sedan, New York license plate number 113-ABT, Vehicle Identification Number 7641239877. She stated that her friend, Ms. Merlin, lives at 1905 Junis Road, her telephone number is 978-4123, she is unmarried, 30 years old, and will return from vacation on November 13. Until then, she can be reached by telephone at 213-804-9112. She is employed at the law firm of Adams and Adams, 360 Park Avenue, as an office manager.

Ms. Graham described the man who stole the car as white, in his early twenties, about 5'7", 155 lbs., and wearing blue pants, a black jacket, and an earring in his left ear. He had dark brown, short curly hair.

Ms. Graham gave her telephone number as 275-8722 and stated that she is divorced, employed as a securities analyst at F.G. Sutton and Company, 125 Wall Street, and is 32 years old. Her birth date is June 13, 1976. Her telephone number at work is 217-7273.

2 (#1)

STOLEN VEHICLE REPORT FORM

COMPLAINT INFORMATION	Complaint Number (1)		Precinct (2)	Date Complaint Reported (3)	Time Reported (4)	Place Complaint Taken (5)
VEHICLE DESCRIPTION	Year (6)		Make (7)	Color (8)		License Number (9)
	I.D. Number (10)		Type (11)		Location of Theft (122)	
OWNER INFORMATION	Name (13)		Address (14)		Home Telephone (15)	
	Age (16)		Marital Status (17)		Occupation (18)	
	Business Address (19)			Business Telephone (20)		
WITNESS INFORMATION	Name (21)		Address (22)		Home Telephone (23)	
	Age (24)		Marital Status (25)		Occupation (26)	
	Business Address (27)			Business Telephone (28)		
	Witness' Description of Incident (29)					
DESCRIPTION OF SUSPECT	Name (If Known) (30)	Age (31)	Race (32)	Sex (33)	Height (34)	Weight (35)	Hair (36)
	Eyes (37)		Clothing (38)		Distinctive Marks (39)	
	Other (40)					
OFFICER INFORMATION	Name (41)			Date (42)		
	Shield Number (43)					

1. Which one of the following should be entered in Box 3?
   A. June 13
   B. October 13
   C. October 30
   D. November 13

2. Which one of the following should be entered in Box 31? 2.____
   A. Late teens   B. Early twenties   C. 30   D. 32

3. Which one of the following should be entered in Box 12? 3.____
   In front of
   A. 1905 Junis Road   B. 523 Johnson Boulevard
   C. 125 Wall Street   D. 360 Park Avenue

4. Which one of the following should be entered in Box 8? 4.____
   A. Blue   B. Brown   C. Black   D. Red

5. Which one of the following should be entered in Box 11? 5.____
   A. 2-door sedan   B. 4-door sedan
   C. 4-door station wagon   D. 2-door sportscar

6. Which one of the following should be entered in Box 15? 6.____
   A. 804-9112   B. 217-7273   C. 275-8722   D. 978-4123

7. Which one of the following should be entered in Box 17? 7.____
   A. Married   B. Legally separated
   C. Single   D. Divorced

8. Which one of the following should be entered in Box 21? 8.____
   A. Samantha Merlin   B. Samantha Graham
   C. Ann Merlin   D. Ann Graham

9. Which one of the following should be entered in Box 26? 9.____
   A. Securities analyst   B. Housewife
   C. Office Manager   D. Secretary

10. Which one of the following should be entered in Box 40? 10.____
    A. Scar on left cheek   B. Earring in left ear
    C. Short curly brown hair   D. Blue pants, black jacket

Questions 11-20.

DIRECTIONS: Questions 11 through 20 are to be answered SOLELY on the basis of the following story and Complaint Report Form.

Officers Fred Johnson and Carl Adams, patrolling in their radio car in the Riverfront section of Precinct #8, were dispatched to 124 Selwyn Lane at 3:23 P.M. on April 26 by the dispatcher. The dispatcher had received a telephone call at 3:20 P.M. from a Mrs. Green who said that her house had been burglarized and all of the contents of her house had been stolen.

Officers Johnson and Adams arrived at 124 Selwyn Lane at 3:28 P.M. Mrs. Green and two neighbors were waiting for them on the front steps. The Officers parked their patrol car in front of the house and locked the doors. Mrs. Green explained that she is a schoolteacher and her husband is a lawyer. They usually leave the house around 8:00 A.M. each morning. She is the first to arrive home since school lets out at 3:00 P.M. She tells the Officers that today, when she arrived home, she found the door to her house slightly open. She was frightened and went to her neighbor's house. Both women then returned to 124 Selwyn and, upon entering the house, found that the contents of the house had been removed. At that point, Mrs. Green called the Police Department.

While Officer Johnson took statements from Mrs. Green and Mrs. Walters, her neighbor, Officer Adams questioned other residents of the street. Most of the other residents were standing outside of the Green's house.

Mrs. Schneider, age 56, who lives 5 doors down at 138 Selwyn, told Officer Adams that she arrived home at 2:45 P.M. She then told Adams that she saw a large truck parked near 124 Selwyn and remembers wondering if anyone new was moving into the neighborhood. She remembers the truck was dented, painted bright blue with a white top, and it had New Jersey plates. Also she was able to describe one of the suspects. She saw him get into the truck before it pulled away. The man was white, about 6'2" tall, about 220 lbs., and thinning brown hair. He was wearing a pair of dirty white overalls and brown work boots. He appeared to walk with a limp. There was another man already in the truck, and Mrs. Schneider described him as a very short Black man wearing a white hat. Mrs. Schneider said the truck turned left on Second Street as it pulled away.

Mrs. Jones, Mrs. Dartnell, and Mrs. Leopold, when questioned by Officer Adams, said that they saw nothing. They were all at Mrs. Leopold's house playing cards and didn't come outside until they heard Mrs. Green screaming.

Officer Adams found that Mrs. Schneider's home phone number was 683-2291 and that she lives alone. Officer Johnson found that both Mrs. Green and her neighbor were 48 years of age and that the school's telephone number was 925-6394. Mrs. Walters' home telephone number is 683-7642, and she lives with her husband at 126 Selwyn Lane. Mr. Green's office number is 238-4296. It is located at 555 Fifth Avenue, Suite 816.

Officers Johnson and Adams then completed the complaint form. The complaint number assigned by the dispatcher was 479638G.

5 (#1)

COMPLAINT REPORT						
COMPLAINT INFORMATION	Complaint Number (1)	Precinct (2)	Date of Complaint (3)	Time of Complaint (4)	Place Complaint Taken (5)	
INFORMATION ABOUT PERSON MAKING COMPLAINT	Name of Person Making Complaint (6) Last Name First Name Middle			Address of Person Making Complaint (7) Street City State			
	Age (8)	Marriage (9) Married ☐ Not-Married ☐		Occupation (If Any) (10)			
	Spouse's Occupation (If Any) (11)			Spouse's Business Address (12) Street City State			
WITNESS INFORMATION	Name of Witness (If Any) (13) Last Name First Name Middle			Address of Witness (If Any) (14) Street City State			
	Age (15)	Occupation (If Any) (16)				
	Spouse's Occupation (If Any) (17)			Spouse's Business Address (18) Street City State			
DESCRIPTION OF INCIDENT	Description (19)					
DESCRIPTION OF SUSPECTS (if Any)	Suspect #1	Name (20)	Age (21)	Race (22) *white*	Sex (23) *male*	Height (24)	Weight (25)	Hair (26)	Eyes (27)
	Suspect #2	Name (28)	Age (29)	Race (30) *black*	Sex (31) *male*	Height (32)	Weight (33)	Hair (34)	Eyes (35)
	Suspect #3	Name (36)	Age (37)	Race (38)	Sex (39)	Height (40)	Weight (41)	Hair (42)	Eyes (43)
	Special Suspect Description (44) Suspect Number _____			Description (45) *Walked with limp*			
SUSPECT VEHICLE DESCRIPTION (If Any)	Year (46)		Make (47)	Color (48)			License Number 49)
OFFICER INFORMATION	Name (50)				Date (51)		
	Shield No. (52)					

11. Which one of the following should be entered in Box 4?   11._____
    A. 8:00 AM   B. 2:45 PM   C. 3:20 PM   D Not known

12. Which one of the following should be entered in Box 6?   12._____
    A. Mrs. Schneider   B. Mrs. Green
    C. Officer Johnson   D. Not known

13. Which one of the following should be entered in Box 7?   13._____
    A. 138 Selwyn Lane   B. 125 Selwyn Lane
    C. 124 Selwyn Lane   D. Not known

14. Which one of the following should be entered in Box 8? 14.____
    A. 48 B. 52 C. 46 D. Not known

15. Which one of the following should be entered in Box 10? 15.____
    A. Lawyer B. Widow C. Teacher D. Not known

16. Which one of the following should be entered in Box 11? 16.____
    A. Lawyer B. Widow C. Teacher D. Not known

17. Which one of the following should be entered in Box 13? 17.____
    A. Mrs. Green B. Mrs. Schneider
    C. Mrs. Leopold D. Not known

18. Which one of the following should be entered in Box 16? 18.____
    A. Lawyer B. Teacher C. Widow D. Not known

19. Which one of the following should be entered in Box 26? 19.____
    A. Black B. Brown C. Blonde D. Not known

20. Which one of the following should be entered in Box 44? 20.____
    A. 1 B. 2 C. 3 D. Not known

KEY (CORRECT ANSWERS)

1.	C	11.	C
2.	B	12.	B
3.	B	13.	C
4.	C	14.	A
5.	A	15.	C
6.	D	16.	A
7.	C	17.	B
8.	D	18.	D
9.	A	19.	B
10.	B	20.	A

TEST 2

DIRECTIONS: Each question or incomplete statement is followed by several suggested answers or completions. Select the one that BEST answers the question or completes the statement. *PRINT THE LETTER OF THE CORRECT ANSWER IN THE SPACE AT THE RIGHT.*

Questions 1-10.

DIRECTIONS: Questions 1 through 10 are to be answered SOLELY on the basis of the following story and Complaint Report Form.

Officers Hunt and Torry respond to a suspected burglary-in-process call at 285 E. Reed Street. They arrive there at 2:32 P.M. A man wearing gray slacks, white dress shirt, and red tie is standing in front of the store yelling, *Stop, robbers!* He is pointing east. Officer Hunt sees three men running about one hundred and fifty feet away. He immediately starts to chase after them. One suspect is 5'9" and weighs about 140 lbs. He has black hair in an Afro cut and is wearing tan pants with a blue work shirt. He is wearing white tennis shoes with blue stripes. He turns the corner and runs south on Elm Street. Another one is 6'2" and weighs about 200 lbs. He has long dark brown hair and is wearing a green headband, white jacket, and blue jeans. He is carrying a brown paper bag in his left hand. He also turns south on Elm. The third man is 5'9" and weighs about 180 lbs. He has long dark brown hair and is wearing a white cap. He is wearing blue jeans and a light blue jacket with a white stripe around it. He continues running east on Reed.

Officer Torry questions the man in the red tie and finds he is the manager of the Elite Jewelry Store and that he has just been robbed by the men running away. Torry radios in the information and continues his questioning. The manager, Mr. Oscar Freehold, says that he was showing a ruby and diamond necklace to Mrs. Mandt, a customer, when these men entered the store. One of them, the tallest one, pointed a gun at Freehold and grabbed the necklace. He put the necklace in the pocket of his white jacket. The other two men were shorter and the same height. The heaver one of the two opened the cash register and emptied the money into a brown paper bag.

The thinner short man opened a display case and put several sapphire and emerald rings in his pants pocket. He then took a knife from his pocket and held it on Mrs. Mandt. The tall one forced Mr. Freehold to open the safe. The tall one took jewels and money from the safe and put them in another brown paper bag. The three men ran out.

Officer Hunt chased the two suspects who turned south on Elm Street. At the next corner, they turned east on Maple. They ran one block to the corner of Beech, where the one with the Afro cut turned south. The other suspect got into a car and drove east on Maple. It was a dark blue 2018 Ford sedan with New York license number 677-HKL. As he drove east on Maple, he sideswiped a 2016 red Dodge and a 2019 tan Volvo.

Officer Hunt returns to the jewelry store and radios in the additional information. Officer Torry completes the Complaint Report.

2 (#2)

COMPLAINT REPORT								
COMPLAINT INFORMATION	Complaint Number (1)	Precinct (2)	Date of Complaint (3)		Time of Complaint (4)	Place Complaint Taken (5)		
INFORMATION ABOUT PERSON MAKING COMPLAINT	Name of Person Making Complaint (6) Last Name First Name Middle					Address of Person Making Complaint (7) Street City State			
	Age (8)	Marriage (9) Married ☐ Not-Married ☐				Occupation (If Any) (10)			
	Spouse's Occupation (If Any) (11)					Spouse's Business Address (12) Street City State			
WITNESS INFORMATION	Name of Witness (If Any) (13) Last Name First Name Middle					Address of Witness (If Any) (14) Street City State			
	Age (15)	Occupation (If Any) (16)								
	Spouse's Occupation (If Any) (17)					Spouse's Business Address (18) Street City State			
DESCRIPTION OF INCIDENT	Description (19)								
DESCRIPTION OF SUSPECTS (if Any)	Suspect #1	Name (20)	Age (21)	Race (22)	Sex (23) *male*	Height (24) 5'9"	Weight (25) 140	Hair (26)	Eyes (27)
	Suspect #2	Name (28)	Age (29)	Race (30) *black*	Sex (31) *male*	Height (32) 6'2"	Weight (33) 200	Hair (34)	Eyes (35)
	Suspect #3	Name (36)	Age (37)	Race (38)	Sex (39) *male*	Height (40) 5'9"	Weight (41) 180	Hair (42)	Eyes (43)
	Special Suspect Description (44) Suspect Number _____					Description (45) *Walked with limp*			
SUSPECT VEHICLE DESCRIPTION (If Any)	Year (46)		Make (47)			Color (48)		License Number 49)	
OFFICER INFORMATION	Name (50)					Date (51)			
	Shield No. (52)							

1. Which of the following should be entered in Box 6?   1.____
   - A. Officer Hunt
   - B. Mr. Oscar Freehold
   - C. Mrs. Mandt
   - D. Not known

2. Which of the following should be entered in Box 10?   2.____
   - A. Jewelry store manager
   - B. Police officer
   - C. Clerk
   - D. Not known

3. Which of the following should be entered in Box 13?   3.____
   - A. Mr. Oscar Freehold
   - B. Mrs. Mandt
   - C. Officer Hunt
   - D. Not known

4. Which of the following should be entered in Box 14?
   A. East Reed Street
   B. East Elm Street
   C. South Beech Street
   D. Not known

5. Which of the following should be entered in Box 26?
   A. Blonde
   B. Brown
   C. Black
   D. Not known

6. Which of the following should be entered in Box 34?
   A. Blonde
   B. Brown
   C. Black
   D. Not known

7. Which of the following should be entered in Box 42?
   A. Blonde
   B. Brown
   C. Black
   D. Not known

8. Which of the following should be entered in Box 46?
   A. 2016
   B. 2018
   C. 2019
   D. Not known

9. Which of the following should be entered in Box 48?
   A. Green
   B. Tan
   C. Blue
   D. Not known

10. Which of the following should be entered in Box 50?
    A. Officer Hunt
    B. Officer Freehold
    C. Officer Torry
    D. Not known

Questions 11-20.

DIRECTIONS: Questions 11 through 20 are to be answered SOLELY on the basis of the following story and Arrest Form.

Officer John Smith, on foot patrol near a delicatessen, heard a man's cry for help. When he reached the man, Peter Laxalt Green, Green told him that he had just been robbed by a young white male who could be seen running down the street. The officer ran after the youth and saw him jump into a 2019 two-door white Buick, New York plate number 761-QCV. While the youth was trying to start the car, the officer caught up with him and arrested him in front of 49 Second Avenue, Brooklyn. The arrest took place ten minutes after the robbery occurred. The officer brought his prisoner to the 65th Precinct station house at 57 Second Avenue, Brooklyn. At the station house, thirty minutes after the robbery, it was determined that the prisoner's legal name was John Wright Doman and his nickname was *Beefy*. Mr. Doman lives at 914 East 140th Street, Brooklyn, Apartment 3G, telephone number 737-1392. He was born in Calgary, Canada, on February 3, 2005. He became a U.S. citizen on February 3, 2012. His Social Security number is 056-46-7056. Doman is not married. He is employed at the Bollero Wine Company, 213 Fourth Avenue, Brooklyn. An arrest report was prepared at the Precinct. The number assigned to the report was 17460.

At the station house, Mr. Green described the incident in detail. Mr. Green stated that at 11:55 P.M. on July 18, 2023, a young, heavy-set white male, 5'11" tall, weighing 220 pounds, with brown hair and blue eyes, entered Mr. Green's delicatessen, at 141 Second Avenue, Brooklyn, New York. Green, who lives in the apartment above the delicatessen, asked him if he could help him. The male replied, *Yes, you can*, and then immediately pulled out a knife. Mr.

4 (#2)

Green then noticed that the male had a red tattoo of an ax on his right arm. The male demanded that Mr. Green give him all the money from the cash register or else Mr. Green would get hurt. Mr. Green picked up a bottle that was on the counter and threw it at the male, striking him in the chest. The male fled from the delicatessen and headed south on Second Avenue. Mr. Green then ran out of the delicatessen and yelled for the police.

Mr. Green was born on March 17, 1969. His business phone number is 871-3113; his home phone number is 330-5286.

ARREST REPORT					
ARREST INFORMATION	Arrest Number (1)	Precinct (2)	Date of Arrest (3)	Time of Arrest (4)	Place of Arrest (5)
DESCRIPTION OF INCIDENT	Date & Time (6)			Prisoner's Weapon (Description (7)	
	Prisoner's Auto (color, year, make, model, license plate number, state) (8)				
	Location of Incident (be specific) (9)			Type of Business (10)	
DESCRIPTION OF PRISONER	Last Name First Name Middle (11)			Date of Birth (12)	
	Age (13)	Sex (14)	Race (15)	Eyes (16)	Hair (17)	Weight (18)	Height (19)
	Address City State			Apt. No. (21)	Home Phone Number (22)
	Place of Birth (23)		Citizenship (24) Citizen ☐ Non-citizen ☐		Marital Status (25)
	Social Security Number (26)		Where Employed (Company and Address) (27)		
	Nickname (28)	Scars, Tattoos (Describe fully and give location) (29)			
DESCRIPTION OF COMPLAINANT	Last Name First Name Middle (30)			Date of Birth (31)	
	Address City State (32)			Telephone Numbers Business: (33) Home: (34)	

11. Which of the following should be entered in Box 3? _____, 2018
    A. February 3   B. March 17   C. July 18   D. July 19

11.____

12. Which of the following should be entered in Box 4?
    A. 11:55 P.M.   B. 12:05 A.M.   C. 12:25 A.M.   D. 12:35 A.M.

12.____

5 (#2)

13. Which of the following should be entered in Box 6? 13.____
    A. 7/18/23, 11:55 P.M.   B. 7/18/23, 11:55 A.M.
    C. 7/19/23, 11:55 P.M.   D. 7/19/23, 11:55 A.M.

14. Which of the following should be entered in Box 7? 14.____
    A. Ax   B. Gun   C. Bottle   D. Knife

15. Which of the following should be entered in Box 8? 15.____
    White _____ Buick, _____, New York
    A. 2019; two-door; 761-QCV   B. 2020; four-door; 762-QCV
    C. 2019; two-door; 761-VCQ   D. 2020; four-door; 167-QCV

16. Which of the following should be entered in Box 12? 16.____
    A. 3/17/69   B. 2/3/05   C. 7/18/05   D. 2/3/12

17. Which of the following should be entered in Box 27? 17.____
    Bollero _____, Brooklyn, N.Y.
    A. Beer Company, 213 Fourth Avenue
    B. Wine Company, 213 Fourth Avenue
    C. Beer & Wine Company, 213 Second Avenue
    D. Wine Company, 213 Fourth Street

18. Which of the following should be entered in Box 32? _____, Brooklyn. 18.____
    A. 49 Second Avenue   B. 57 Second Avenue
    C. 141 Second Avenue   D. 914 East 140th Street

19. Which of the following should be entered in Box 33? 19.____
    A. 330-1392   B. 330-5286   C. 737-1392   D. 871-3113

20. Which of the following should be entered in Box 28? 20.____
    A. Doman   B. Axe   C. Beefy   D. Maniac

KEY (CORRECT ANSWERS)

1.	B	11.	D
2.	A	12.	B
3.	B	13.	A
4.	D	14.	D
5.	C	15.	A
6.	B	16.	B
7.	B	17.	B
8.	B	18.	C
9.	C	19.	D
10.	C	20.	C

PREPARING WRITTEN MATERIALS

EXAMINATION SECTION

TEST 1

DIRECTIONS: Each question consists of a sentence which may be classified appropriately under one of the following four categories:
- A. Incorrect because of faulty grammar or sentence structure.
- B. Incorrect because of faulty punctuation.
- C. Incorrect because of faulty spelling or capitalization.
- D. Correct

Examine each sentence carefully. Then, in the space at the right, print the capital letter preceding the option which is the BEST of the four suggested above. All incorrect sentences contain only one type of error. Consider a sentence correct if it contains none of the types of errors mentioned, although there may be other correct ways of expressing the same thought.

1. The fire apparently started in the storeroom, which is usually locked. 1.____
2. On approaching the victim two bruises were noticed by this officer. 2.____
3. The officer, who was there examined the report with great care. 3.____
4. Each employee in the office had a separate desk. 4.____
5. The suggested procedure is similar to the one now in use. 5.____
6. No one was more pleased with the new procedure than the chauffeur. 6.____
7. He tried to pursuade her to change the procedure. 7.____
8. The total of the expenses charged to petty cash were high. 8.____
9. An understanding between him and I was finally reached. 9.____
10. It was at the supervisor's request that the clerk agreed to postpone his vacation. 10.____
11. We do not believe that it is necessary for both he and the clerk to attend the conference. 11.____
12. All employees, who display perseverance, will be given adequate recognition. 12.____
13. He regrets that some of us employees are dissatisfied with our new assignments. 13.____

14. "Do you think that the raise was merited," asked the supervisor? 14._____

15. The new manual of procedure is a valuable supplament to our rules and regulation. 15._____

16. The typist admitted that she had attempted to pursuade the other employees to assist her in her work. 16._____

17. The supervisor asked that all amendments to the regulations be handled by you and I. 17._____

18. They told both he and I that the prisoner had escaped. 18._____

19. Any superior officer, who, disregards the just complaints of his subordinates, is remiss in the performance of his duty. 19._____

20. Only those members of the national organization who resided in the Middle west attended the conference in Chicago. 20._____

21. We told him to give the investigation assignment to whoever was available. 21._____

22. Please do not disappoint and embarass us by not appearing in court. 22._____

23. Despite the efforts of the Supervising mechanic, the elevator could not be started. 23._____

24. The U.S. Weather Bureau, weather record for the accident date was checked. 24._____

KEY (CORRECT ANSWERS)

1.	D	11.	A
2.	A	12.	B
3.	B	13.	D
4.	D	14.	B
5.	D	15.	C
6.	D	16.	C
7.	C	17.	A
8.	A	18.	A
9.	A	19.	B
10.	D	20.	C
21.	D		
22.	C		
23.	C		
24.	B		

TEST 2

DIRECTIONS: Each question consists of a sentence. Some of the sentences contain errors in English grammar or usage, punctuation, spelling, or capitalization. A sentence does not contain an error simply because it could be written in a different manner. Choose answer:
   A. If the sentence contains an error in English grammar or usage.
   B. if the sentence contains an error in punctuation.
   C. If the sentence contains an error in spelling or capitalization
   D. If the sentence does not contain any errors.

1. The severity of the sentence prescribed by contemporary statutes—including both the former and the revised New York Penal Laws—do not depend on what crime was intended by the offender.

2. It is generally recognized that two defects in the early law of attempt played a part in the birth of burglary: (1) immunity from prosecution for conduct short of the last act before completion of the crime, and (2) the relatively minor penalty imposed for an attempt (it being a common law misdemeanor) vis-à-vis the completed offense.

3. The first sentence of the statute is applicable to employees who enter their place of employment, invited guests, and all other persons who have an express or implied license or privilege to enter the premises.

4. Contemporary criminal codes in the United States generally divide burglary into various degrees, differentiating the categories according to place, time and other attendent circumstances.

5. The assignment was completed in record time but the payroll for it has not yet been prepaid.

6. The operator, on the other hand, is willing to learn me how to use the mimeograph.

7. She is the prettiest of the three sisters.

8. She doesn't know; if the mail has arrived.

9. The doorknob of the office door is broke.

10. Although the department's supply of scratch pads and stationery have diminished considerably, the allotment for our division has not been reduced.

11. You have not told us whom you wish to designate as your secretary.

12. Upon reading the minutes of the last meeting, the new proposal was taken up for consideration.

13. Before beginning the discussion, we locked the door as a precautionery measure. 13.____

14. The supervisor remarked, "Only those clerks, who perform routine work, are permitted to take a rest period." 14.____

15. Not only will this duplicating machine make accurate copies, but it will also produce a quantity of work equal to fifteen transcribing typists. 15.____

16. "Mr. Jones," said the supervisor, "we regret our inability to grant you an extention of your leave of absence." 16.____

17. Although the employees find the work monotonous and fatigueing, they rarely complain. 17.____

18. We completed the tabulation of the receipts on time despite the fact that Miss Smith our fastest operator was absent for over a week. 18.____

19. The reaction of the employees who attended the meeting, as well as the reaction of those who did not attend, indicates clearly that the schedule is satisfactory to everyone concerned. 19.____

20. Of the two employees, the one in our office is the most efficient. 20.____

21. No one can apply or even understand, the new rules and regulations. 21.____

22. A large amount of supplies were stored in the empty office. 22.____

23. If an employee is occassionally asked to work overtime, he should do so willingly. 23.____

24. It is true that the new procedures are difficult to use but, we are certain that you will learn them quickly. 24.____

25. The office manager said that he did not know who would be given a large allotment under the new plan. 25.____

KEY (CORRECT ANSWERS)

1. A
2. D
3. D
4. C
5. C

6. A
7. D
8. B
9. A
10. A

11. D
12. A
13. C
14. B
15. A

16. C
17. C
18. B
19. D
20. A

21. B
22. A
23. C
24. B
25. D

TEST 3

DIRECTIONS: Each of the following sentences may be classified MOST appropriately under one of the following categories:
A. Faulty because of incorrect grammar
B. Faulty because of incorrect punctuation
C. Faulty because of incorrect capitalization
D. Correct

Examine each sentence carefully. Then, in the space at the right, print the capital letter preceding the option which is the BEST of the four suggested above. All incorrect sentence contain but one type of error. Consider a sentence correct if it contains none of the types of errors mentioned, even though there may be other correct ways of expressing the same thought.

1. The desk, as well as the chairs, were moved out of the office. 1._____

2. The clerk whose production was greatest for the month won a day's vacation as first prize. 2._____

3. Upon entering the room, the employees were found hard at work at their desks. 3._____

4. John Smith our new employee always arrives at work on time. 4._____

5. Punish whoever is guilty of stealing the money. 5._____

6. Intelligent and persistent effort lead to success no matter what the job may be. 6._____

7. The secretary asked, "can you call again at three o'clock?" 7._____

8. He told us, that if the report was not accepted at the next meeting, it would have to be rewritten. 8._____

9. He would not have sent the letter if he had known that it would cause so much excitement. 9._____

10. We all looked forward to him coming to visit us. 10._____

11. If you find that you are unable to complete the assignment please notify me as soon as possible. 11._____

12. Every girl in the office went home on time but me; there was still some work for me to finish. 12._____

13. He wanted to know who the letter was addressed to, Mr. Brown or Mr. Smith. 13._____

14. "Mr. Jones, he said, please answer this letter as soon as possible." 14._____

15. The new clerk had an unusual accent inasmuch as he was born and educated in the south.

16. Although he is younger than her, he earns a higher salary.

17. Neither of the two administrators are going to attend the conference being held in Washington, D.C.

18. Since Miss Smith and Miss Jones have more experience than us, they have been given more responsible duties.

19. Mr. Shaw the supervisor of the stock room maintains an inventory of stationery and office supplies.

20. Inasmuch as this matter affects both you and I, we should take joint action.

21. Who do you think will be able to perform this highly technical work?

22. Of the two employees, John is considered the most competent.

23. He is not coming home on tuesday; we expect him next week.

24. Stenographers, as well as typists must be able to type rapidly and accurately.

25. Having been placed in the safe we were sure that the money would not be stolen.

15.____
16.____
17.____
18.____
19.____
20.____
21.____
22.____
23.____
24.____
25.____

KEY (CORRECT ANSWERS)

1.	A	11.	B
2.	D	12.	D
3.	A	13.	A
4.	B	14.	B
5.	D	15.	C
6.	A	16.	A
7.	C	17.	A
8.	B	18.	A
9.	D	19.	B
10.	A	20.	A

21. D
22. A
23. C
24. B
25. A

TEST 4

DIRECTIONS: Each of the following sentences consist of four sentences lettered A, B, C, and D. One of the sentences in each group contains an error in grammar or punctuation. Indicate the INCORRECT sentence in each group. *PRINT THE LETTER OF THE CORRECT ANSWER IN THE SPACE AT THE RIGHT.*

1. A. Give the message to whoever is on duty.
   B. The teacher who's pupil won first prize presented the award.
   C. Between you and me, I don't expect the program to succeed.
   D. His running to catch the bus caused the accident.

1.____

2. A. The process, which was patented only last year is already obsolete.
   B. His interest in science (which continues to the present) led him to convert his basement into a laboratory.
   C. He described the book as "verbose, repetitious, and bombastic".
   D. Our new director will need to possess three qualities: vision, patience, and fortitude.

2.____

3. A. The length of ladder trucks varies considerably.
   B. The probationary fireman reported to the officer to who he was assigned.
   C. The lecturer emphasized the need for we firemen to be punctual.
   D. Neither the officers nor the members of the company knew about the new procedure.

3.____

4. A. Ham and eggs is the specialty of the house.
   B. He is one of the students who are on probation.
   C. Do you think that either one of us have a chance to be nominated for president of the class?
   D. I assume that either he was to be in charge or you were.

4.____

5. A. Its a long road that has no turn.
   B. To run is more tiring than to walk.
   C. We have been assigned three new reports: namely, the statistical summary, the narrative summary, and the budgetary summary.
   D. Had the first payment been made in January, the second would be due in April.

5.____

6. A. Each employer has his own responsibilities.
   B. If a person speaks correctly, they make a good impression.
   C. Every one of the operators has had her vacation.
   D. Has anybody filed his report?

6.____

7. A. The manager, with all his salesmen, was obliged to go.
   B. Who besides them is to sign the agreement?
   C. One report without the others is incomplete.
   D. Several clerks, as well as the proprietor, was injured.

7.____

8. A. A suspension of these activities is expected.
    B. The machine is economical because first cost and upkeep are low.
    C. A knowledge of stenography and filing are required for this position.
    D. The condition in which the goods were received shows that the packing was not done properly.

9. A. There seems to be a great many reasons for disagreement.
    B. It does not seem possible that they could have failed.
    C. Have there always been too few applicants for these positions?
    D. There is no excuse for these errors.

10. A. We shall be pleased to answer your question.
    B. Shall we plan the meeting for Saturday?
    C. I will call you promptly at seven.
    D. Can I borrow your book after you have read it?

11. A. You are as capable as I.
    B. Everyone is willing to sign but him and me.
    C. As for he and his assistant, I cannot praise them too highly.
    D. Between you and me, I think he will be dismissed.

12. A. Our competitors bid above us last week.
    B. The survey which was began last year has not yet been completed.
    C. The operators had shown that they understood their instructions.
    D. We have never ridden over worse roads.

13. A. Who did they say was responsible?
    B. Whom did you suspect?
    C. Who do you suppose it was?
    D. Whom do you mean?

14. A. Of the two propositions, this is the worse.
    B. Which report do you consider the best—the one in January or the one in July?
    C. I believe this is the most practicable of the many plans submitted.
    D. He is the youngest employee in the organization.

15. A. The firm had but three orders last week.
    B. That doesn't really seem possible.
    C. After twenty years scarcely none of the old business remains.
    D. Has he done nothing about it?

KEY (CORRECT ANSWERS)

1. B
2. A
3. C
4. C
5. A
6. B
7. D
8. C
9. A
10. D
11. C
12. B
13. A
14. B
15. C

PREPARING WRITTEN MATERIAL

PARAGRAPH REARRANGEMENT
COMMENTARY

The sentences that follow are in scrambled order. You are to rearrange them in proper order and indicate the letter choice containing the correct answer at the space at the right.

Each group of sentences in this section is actually a paragraph presented in scrambled order. Each sentence in the group has a place in that paragraph; no sentence is to be left out. You are to read each group of sentences and decide upon the best order in which to put the sentences so as to form a well-organized paragraph.

The questions in this section measure the ability to solve a problem when all the facts relevant to its solution are not given.

More specifically, certain positions of responsibility and authority require the employee to discover connection between events sometimes, apparently, unrelated. In order to do this, the employee will find it necessary to correctly infer that unspecified events have probably occurred or are likely to occur. This ability becomes especially important when action must be taken on incomplete information.

Accordingly, these questions require competitors to choose among several suggested alternatives, each of which presents a different sequential arrangement of the events. Competitors must choose the MOST logical of the suggested sequences.

In order to do so, they may be required to draw on general knowledge to infer missing concepts or events that are essential to sequencing the given events. Competitors should be careful to infer only what is essential to the sequence. The plausibility of the wrong alternatives will always require the inclusion of unlikely events or of additional chains of events which are NOT essential to sequencing the given events.

It's very important to remember that you are looking for the best of the four possible choices, and that the best choice of all may not even be one of the answers you're given to choose from.

There is no one right way to solve these problems. Many people have found it helpful to first write out the order of the sentences, as they would have arranged them, on their scrap paper before looking at the possible answers. If their optimum answer is there, this can save them some time. If it isn't, this method can still give insight into solving the problem. Others find it most helpful to just go through each of the possible choices, contrasting each as they go along. You should use whatever method feels comfortable and works for you.

While most of these types of questions are not that difficult, we've added a higher percentage of the difficult type, just to give you more practice. Usually there are only one or two questions on this section that contain such subtle distinctions that you're unable to answer confidently. And you then may find yourself stuck deciding between two possible choices, neither of which you're sure about.

PREPARING WRITTEN MATERIAL
PARAGRAPH REARRANGEMENT

EXAMINATION SECTION

TEST 1

DIRECTIONS: The sentences that follow are in scrambled order. You are to rearrange them in proper order and indicate the letter choice containing the CORRECT answer. *PRINT THE LETTER OF THE CORRECT ANSWER IN THE SPACE AT THE RIGHT.*

1. Police Officer Jenner responds to the scene of a burglary at 2106 La Vista Boulevard. He is approached by an elderly man named Richard Jenkins, whose account of the incident includes the following five sentences:
   I. I saw that the lock on my apartment door had been smashed and the door was open.
   II. My apartment was a shambles; my belongings were everywhere and my television set was missing.
   III. As I walked down the hallway toward the bedroom, I heard someone opening a window.
   IV. I left work at 5:30 P.M. and took the bus home.
   V. At that time, I called the police.
   The MOST logical order for the above sentence to appear in the report is
   A. I, V, IV, II, III   B. IV, I, II, III, V   C. I, V, II, III, IV   D. IV, III, II, V, I

1.____

2. Police Officer LaJolla is writing an Incident Report in which back-up assistance was required. The report will contain the following five sentences:
   I. The radio dispatcher asked what my location was and he then dispatched patrol cars for back-up assistance.
   II. At approximately 9:30 P.M., while I was walking my assigned footpost, a gunman fired three shots at me.
   III. I quickly turned around and saw a white male, approximately 5'10", with black hair, wearing blue jeans, a yellow T-shirt, and white sneaker, running across the avenue carrying a handgun.
   IV. When the back-up officers arrived, we searched the area but could not find the suspect.
   V. I advised the radio dispatcher that a gunman had just fired a gun at me, and then I gave the dispatcher a description of the man
   The MOST logical order for the above sentences to appear in the report is:
   A. III, V, II, IV, I   B. II, III, V, I, IV   C. III, II, IV, I, V   D. II, V, I, III, IV

2.____

3. Police Officer Durant is completing a report of a robbery and assault. The report will contain the following five sentences:
   I. I went to Mount Snow Hospital to interview a man who was attacked and robbed of his wallet earlier that night.
   II. An ambulance arrived at 82nd Street and 3rd Avenue and took an intoxicated, wounded man to Mount Snow Hospital
   III. Two youths attacked the man and stole his wallet.

3.____

IV. A well-dressed man left Hanratty's Bar very drunk, with his wallet hanging out of his back pocket.
V. A passerby dialed 911 and requested police and ambulance assistance.
The MOST logical order for the above sentences to appear in the report is
   A. I, II, IV, III, V   B. IV, III, V, II, I   C. IV, V, II, III, I   D. V, IV, III, II, I

4. Police Officer Boswell is preparing a report of an armed robbery and assault which will contain the following five sentences:
   I. Both men approached the bartender and one of them drew a gun.
   II. The bartender immediately went to grab the phone at the bar.
   III. One of the men leaped over the counter and smashed a bottle over the bartender's head.
   IV. Two men in a blue Buick drove up to the bar and went inside.
   V. I found the cash register empty and the bartender unconscious on the floor, with the phone still dangling off the hook.
   The MOST logical order for the above sentences to appear in the report is
      A. IV, I, II, II, V   B. V, IV, III, I, II   C. IV, III, II, V, I   D. II, I, III, IV, V

5. Police Officer Mitzler is preparing a report of a bank robbery, which will contain the following five sentences:
   I. The teller complied with the instructions on the note, but also hit the silent alarm.
   II. The perpetrator then fled south on Broadway.
   III. A suspicious male entered the bank at approximately 10:45 A.M.
   IV. At this time, an undetermined amount of money has been taken.
   V. He approached the teller on the far right side and handed her a note.
   The MOST logical order for the above sentences to appear in the report is:
      A. III, V, I, II, IV   B. I, III, V, II, IV   C. III, V, IV, I, II   D. III, V, II, IV, I

6. A Police Officer is preparing an Accident Report for an accident which occurred at the intersection of East 119th Street and Lexington Avenue. The report will include the following five sentences:
   I. On September 18, while driving ten children to school, a school bus driver passed out.
   II. Upon arriving at the scene, I notified the dispatcher to send an ambulance.
   III. I notified the parents of each child once I got to the station house.
   IV. He said the school bus, while traveling west on East 119th Street, struck a parked Ford which was on the southwest corner of East 119th Street.
   V. A witness by the name of John Ramos came up to me to describe what happened.
   The MOST logical order for the above sentences to appear in the Accident Report is:
      A. I, II, V, III, IV   B. I, II, V, IV, III   C. II, V, I, III, IV   D. II, V, I, IV, III

7. A Police Officer is preparing a report concerning a dispute. The report will contain the following five sentences:
   I. The passenger got out of the back of the taxi and leaned through the front window to complain to the driver about the fare.

II. The driver of the taxi caught up with the passenger and knocked him to the ground; the passenger then kicked the driver and a scuffle ensued.
III. The taxi drew up in front of the high-rise building and stopped.
IV. The driver got out of the taxi and followed the passenger into the lobby of the apartment building.
V. The doorman tried but was unable to break up the fight, at which point he called the precinct.

The MOST logical order for the above sentences to appear in the report is
   A. III, I, IV, II, V   B. III, IV, I, II, V   C. III, IV, II, V, I   D. V, I, III, IV, II

8. Police Officer Morrow is writing an Incident Report. The report will include the following four sentences:
   I. The man reached into his pocket and pulled out a gun.
   II. While on foot patrol, I identified a suspect, who was wanted for six robberies in the area, from a wanted picture I was carrying.
   III. I drew my weapon and fired six rounds at the suspect, killing him instantly.
   IV. I called for back-up assistance and told the man to put his hands up.

   The MOST logical order for the above sentences to appear in the report is
      A. II, III, IV, I   B. IV, I, III, II   C. IV, I, II, III   D. II, IV, I, III

9. Sergeant Allen responds to a call at 16 Grove Street regarding a missing child. At the scene, the Sergeant is met by Police Officer Samuels, who gives a brief account of the incident consisting of the following five sentences:
   I. I transmitted the description and waited for you to arrive before I began searching the area.
   II. Mrs. Banks, the mother, reports that she last saw her daughter Julie about 7:30 A.M. when she took her to school.
   III. About 6 P.M., my partner and I arrived at this location to investigate a report of a missing 8-year-old girl.
   IV. When Mrs. Banks left her, Julie was wearing a red and white striped T-shirt, blue jeans, and white sneakers.
   V. Mrs. Banks dropped her off in front of the playground of P.S. 11.

   The MOST logical order for the above sentences to appear in the report is
      A. III, V, IV, II, I   B. III, II, V, IV, I   C. III, IV, I, II, V   D. III, II, IV, I, V

10. Police Officer Franco is completing a report of an assault. The report will contain the following five sentences:
    I. In the park I observed an elderly man lying on the ground, bleeding from a back wound.
    II. I applied first aid to control the bleeding and radioed for an ambulance to respond.
    III. The elderly man stated that he was sitting on the park bench when he was attacked from behind by two males.
    IV. I received a report of a man's screams coming from inside the park, and I went to investigate.
    V. The old man could not give a description of his attackers.

    The MOST logical order for the above sentences to appear in the report is
       A. IV, I, II, III, V   B. V, III, I, IV, II   C. IV, III, V, II, I   D. II, I, V, IV, III

11. Police Officer Williams is completing a Crime Report. The report contains the following five sentences:
    I. As Police Officer Hanson and I approached the store, we noticed that the front door was broken.
    II. After determining that the burglars had fled, we notified the precinct of the burglary.
    III. I walked through the front door as Police Officer Hanson walked around to the back.
    IV. At approximately midnight, an alarm was heard at the Apex Jewelry Store.
    V. We searched the store and found no one.
    The MOST logical order for the above sentences to appear in the report is
       A. I, IV, II, III, V   B. I, IV, III, V, II   C. IV, I, III, II, V   D. IV, I, III, V, II

    11.____

12. Police Officer Clay is giving a report to the news media regarding someone who has jumped from the Empire State Building. His report will include the following five sentences:
    I. I responded to the 86th floor, where I found the person at the edge of the roof.
    II. A security guard at the building had reported that a man was on the roof at the 86th floor.
    III. At 5:30 P.M., the person jumped from the building.
    IV. I received a call from the radio dispatcher at 4:50 P.M. to respond to the Empire State Building.
    V. I tried to talk to the person and convince him not to jump.
    The MOST logical order for the above sentences to appear in the report is
       A. I, II, IV, III, V   B. III, IV, I, II, V   C. II, IV, I, III, V   D. IV, II, I, V, III

    12.____

13. The following five sentences are part of a report of a burglary written by Police Officer Reed:
    I. When I arrived at 2400 1st Avenue, I noticed that the door was slightly open.
    II. I yelled out, *Police, don't move!*
    III. As I entered the apartment, I saw a man with a TV set passing through a window to another man standing on a fire escape.
    IV. While on foot patrol, I was informed by the radio dispatcher that a burglary was in progress at 2400 1st Avenue.
    V. However, the burglars quickly ran down the fire escape.
    The MOST logical order for the above sentences to appear in the report is
       A. I, III, IV, V, II   B. IV, I, III, V, II   C. IV, I, III, II, V   D. I, IV, III, II, V

    13.____

14. Police Officer Jenkins is preparing a report for Lost or Stolen Property. The report will include the following five sentences:
    I. On the stairs, Mr. Harris slipped on a wet leaf and fell on the landing.
    II. It wasn't until he got to the token booth that Mr. Harris realized his wallet was no longer in his back pants pocket.
    III. A boy wearing a football jersey helped him up and brushed off the back of Mr. Harris' pants.
    IV. Mr. Harris states he was walking up the stairs to the elevated subway at Queensborough Plaza.
    V. Before Mr. Harris could thank him, the boy was running down the stairs to the street.

    14.____

The MOST logical order for the above sentences to appear in the report is
A. IV, III, V, I, II B. IV, I, III, V, II C. I, IV, II, III, V D. I, II, IV, III, V

15. Police Officer Hubbard is completing a report of a missing person. The report will contain the following five sentences:
    I. I visited the store at 7:55 P.M. and asked the employees if they had seen a girl fitting the description I had been given.
    II. She gave me a description and said she had gone into the local grocery store at about 6:15 P.M.
    III. I asked the woman for a description of her daughter.
    IV. The distraught woman called the precinct to report that her daughter, aged 12, had not returned from an errand.
    V. The storekeeper said a girl matching the description had been in the store earlier, but he could not give an exact time.
    The MOST logical order for the above sentences to appear in the report is
    A. I, III, II, V, IV B. IV, III, II, I, V C. V, I, II, III, IV D. III, I, II, IV, V

16. A police officer is completing an entry in his Daily Activity Log regarding traffic summonses which he issued. The following five sentences will be included in the entry:
    I. I was on routine patrol parked 16 yards west of 170th Street and Clay Avenue.
    II. The summonses were issued for unlicensed operator and disobeying a steady red light.
    III. At 8 A.M. hours, I observed an auto traveling westbound on 170th Street not stop for a steady red light at the intersection of Clay Avenue and 170th Street.
    IV. I stopped the driver of the auto and determined that he did not have a valid driver's license.
    V. After a brief conversation, I informed the motorist that he was receiving two summonses.
    The MOST logical order for the above sentences to appear in the report is
    A. I, III, IV, V, II B. III, IV, II, V, I C. V, II, I, III, IV D. IV, V, II, I, III

17. The following sentences appeared on an Incident Report:
    I. Three teenagers who had been ejected from the theater were yelling at patrons who were now entering.
    II. Police Officer Dixon told the teenagers to leave the area.
    III. The teenager said that they were told by the manager to leave the theater because they were talking during the movie.
    IV. The theater manager called the precinct at 10:20 P.M. to report a disturbance outside the theater.
    V. A patrol car responded to the theater at 10:42 P.M. and two police officers went over to the teenagers.
    The MOST logical order for the above sentences to appear in the Incident Report is
    A. I, V, IV, III, II B. IV, I, V, III, II C. IV, I, III, V, II D. IV, III, I, V, II

18. Activity Log entries are completed by police officers. Police Officer Samuels has written an entry concerning vandalism and part of it contains the following five sentences:
    I. The man, in his early twenties, ran down the block and around the corner.
    II. A man passing the store threw a brick through a window of the store.
    III. I arrived on the scene and began to question the witnesses about the incident.
    IV. Malcolm Holmes, the owner of the Fast Service Shoe Repair Store, was working in the back of the store at approximately 3 P.M.
    V. After the man fled, Mr. Holmes called the police.
    The MOST logical order for the above sentences to appear in the Activity Log is
    A. IV, II, I, V, III   B. II, IV, I, III, V   C. II, I, IV, III, V   D. IV, II, V, III, I

19. Police Officer Buckley is preparing a report concerning a dispute in a restaurant. The report will contain the following five sentences:
    I. The manager, Charles Chin, and a customer, Edward Green, were standing near the register arguing over the bill.
    II. The manager refused to press any charges providing Green pay the check and leave.
    III. While on foot patrol, I was informed by a passerby of a disturbance in the Dragon Flame Restaurant.
    IV. Green paid the $15.00 check and left the restaurant.
    V. According to witnesses, the customer punched the owner in the face when Chin asked him for the amount due.
    The MOST logical order for the above sentences to appear in the report is
    A. III, I, V, II, IV   B. I, II, III, IV, V   C. V, I, III, II, IV   D. III, V, II, IV, I

20. Police Officer Wilkins is preparing a report for leaving the scene of an accident. The report will include the following five sentences:
    I. The Dodge struck the right rear fender of Mrs. Smith's 2010 Ford and continued on its way.
    II. Mrs. Smith stated she was making a left turn from 40th Street onto Third Avenue.
    III. As the car passed, Mrs. Smith noticed the dangling rear license plate #412AEJ.
    IV. Mrs. Smith complained to police of back pains and was removed by ambulance to Bellevue Hospital.
    V. An old green Dodge traveling up Third Avenue went through the red light at 40th Street and Third Avenue.
    The MOST logical order for the above sentences to appear in the report is
    A. V, III, I, II, IV   B. I, III, II, V, IV   C. IV, V, I, II, III   D. II, V, I, III, IV

21. Detective Simon is completing a Crime Report. The report contains the following five sentences:
    I. Police Officer Chin, while on foot patrol, heard the yelling and ran in the direction of the man.
    II. The man, carrying a large hunting knife, left the High Sierra Sporting Goods Store at approximately 10:30 A.M.

III. When the man heard Police Officer Chin, he stopped, dropped the knife, and began to cry.
IV. As Police Officer Chin approached the man, he drew his gun and yelled, *Police, freeze.*
V. After the man left the store, he began yelling, over and over, *I am going to kill myself!*

The MOST logical order for the above sentences to appear in the report is
A. V, II, I, IV, III B. II, V, I, IV, III C. II, V, IV, I, III D. II, I, V, IV, III

22. Police Officer Miller is preparing a Complaint Report which will include the following five sentences:
   I. From across the lot, he yelled to the boys to get away from his car.
   II. When he came out of the store, he noticed two teenage boys trying to break into his car.
   III. The boys fled as Mr. Johnson ran to his car.
   IV. Mr. Johnson stated that he parked his car in the municipal lot behind Tams Department Store.
   V. Mr. Johnson saw that the door lock had been broken, but nothing was missing from inside the auto.

   The MOST logical order for the above sentences to appear in the report is
   A. IV, I, II, V, III B. II, III, I, V, IV C. IV, II, I, III, V D. I, II, III, V, IV

23. Police Officer O'Hara completes a Universal Summons for a motorist who has just passed a red traffic light. The Universal Summons includes the following five sentences:
   I. As the car passed the light, I followed in the patrol car.
   II. After the driver stopped the car, he stated that the light was yellow, not red.
   III. A blue Cadillac sedan passed the red light on the corner of 79th Street and 3rd Avenue at 11:25 P.M.
   IV. As a result, the driver was informed that he did pass a red light and that his brake lights were not working.
   V. The driver in the Cadillac stopped his car as soon as he saw the patrol car, and I noticed that the brake lights were not working.

   The MOST logical order for the above sentences to appear in the Universal Summons is
   A. I, III, V, II, IV B. III, I, V, II, IV C. III, I, V, IV, II D. I, III, IV, II, V

24. Detective Egan is preparing a follow-up report regarding a homicide on 170th Street and College Avenue. An unknown male was found at the scene. The report will contain the following five sentences:
   I. Police Officer Gregory wrote down the names, addresses, and phone numbers of the witnesses.
   II. A 911 operator received a call of a man shot and dispatched Police Officers Worth and Gregory to the scene.
   III. They discovered an unidentified male dead on the street.
   IV. Police Officer Worth notified the Precinct Detective Unit immediately.
   V. At approximately 9:00 A.M., an unidentified male shot another male in the chest during an argument.

The MOST logical order for the above sentences to appear in the report is
A. V, II, III, IV, I B. II, III, V, IV, I C. IV, I, V, II, III D. V, III, II, IV, I

25. Police Officer Tracey is preparing a Robbery Report which will include the following five sentences:
I. I ran around the corner and observe a man pointing a gun at a taxidriver.
II. I informed the man I was a police officer and that he should not move.
III. I was on the corner of 125th Street and Park Avenue when I heard a scream coming from around the corner.
IV. The man turned around and fired one shot at me.
V. I fired once, shooting him in the arm and causing him to fall to the ground.
The MOST logical order for the above sentences to appear in the report is
A. I, III, IV, II, V B. IV, V, II, I, III C. III, I, II, IV, V D. III, I, V, II, IV

KEY (CORRECT ANSWERS)

1.	B		11.	D
2.	B		12.	D
3.	B		13.	C
4.	A		14.	B
5.	A		15.	B
6.	B		16.	A
7.	A		17.	B
8.	D		18.	A
9.	B		19.	A
10.	A		20.	D

21.	B
22.	C
23.	B
24.	A
25.	C

TEST 2

DIRECTIONS: The sentences that follow are in scrambled order. You are to rearrange them in proper order and indicate the letter choice containing the CORRECT answer. *PRINT THE LETTER OF THE CORRECT ANSWER IN THE SPACE AT THE RIGHT*

1. Police Officer Weiker is completing a Complaint Report which will contain the following five sentences: 1.____
   I. Mr. Texlor was informed that the owner of the van would receive a parking ticket and that the van would be towed away.
   II. The police tow truck arrived approximately one half hour after Mr. Texlor complained.
   III. While on foot patrol on West End Avenue, I saw the owner of Rand's Restaurant arrive to open his business.
   IV. Mr. Texlor, the owner, called to me and complained that he could not receive deliveries because a van was blocking his driveway.
   V. The van's owner later reported to the precinct that his van had been stolen, and he was then informed that it had been towed.
   The MOST logical order for the above sentences to appear in the report is
      A. III, V, I, II, IV   B. III, IV, I, II, V   C. IV, III, I, II, V   D. IV, III, II, I, V

2. Police Officer Ames is completing an entry in his Activity Log. The entry contains the following five sentences: 2.____
   I. Mr. Sands gave me a complete description of the robber.
   II. Alvin Sands, owner of the Star Delicatessen, called the precinct to report he had just been robbed.
   III. I then notified all police patrol vehicles to look for a white male in his early twenties wearing brown pants and shirt, a black leather jacket, and black and white sneakers.
   IV. I arrived on the scene after being notified by the precinct that a robbery had just occurred at the Star Delicatessen.
   V. Twenty minutes later, a man fitting the description was arrested by a police officer on patrol six blocks from the delicatessen.
   The MOST logical order for the above sentences to appear in the Activity Log is
      A. II, I, IV, III, V   B. II IV, III, I, V   C. II, IV, I, III, V   D. II, IV, I, V, III

3. Police Officer Benson is completing a Complaint Report concerning a stolen taxicab, which will include the following five sentences: 3.____
   I. Police Officer Benson noticed that a cab was parked next to a fire hydrant.
   II. Dawson *borrowed* the cab for transportation purposes since he was in a hurry.
   III. Ed Dawson got into his car and tried to start it, but the battery was dead.
   IV. When he reached his destination, he parked the cab by a fire hydrant and placed the keys under the seat.
   V. He looked around and saw an empty cab with the engine running.
   The MOST logical order for the above sentences to appear in the report is
      A. I, III, II, IV, V   B. III, I, II, V, IV   C. III, V, II, IV, I   D. V, II, IV, III, I

4. Police Officer Hatfield is reviewing his Activity Log entry prior to completing a report. The entry contains the following five sentences:
   I. When I arrived at Zand's Jewelry Store, I noticed that the door was slightly open.
   II. I told the burglar I was a police officer and that he should stand still or he would be shot.
   III. As I entered the store, I saw a man wearing a ski mask attempting to open the safe in the back of the store.
   IV. On December 16, 2020, at 1:38 A.M., I was informed that a burglary was in progress at Zand's Jewelry Store on East 59th Street.
   V. The burglar quickly pulled a knife from his pocket when he saw me.
   The MOST logical order for the above sentences to appear in the report is
   A. IV, I, III, V, II   B. I, IV, III, V, II   C. IV, III, II, V, I   D. I, III, IV, V, II

5. Police Officer Lorenz is completing a report of a murder. The report will contain the following five statements made by a witness:
   I. I was awakened by the sound of a gunshot coming from the apartment next door and I decided to check.
   II. I entered the apartment and looked into the kitchen and the bathroom.
   III. I found Mr. Hubbard's body slumped in the bathtub.
   IV. The door to the apartment was open, but I didn't see anyone.
   V. He had been shot in the head.
   The MOST logical order for the above sentences to appear in the report is
   A. I, III, II, IV, V   B. I, IV, II, III, V   C. IV, II, I, III, V   D. III, I, II, IV, V

6. Police Officer Baldwin is preparing an accident report which will include the following five sentences:
   I. The old man lay on the ground for a few minutes, but was not physically hurt.
   II. Charlie Watson, a construction worker, was repairing some brick work at the top of a building at 54th Street and Madison Avenue.
   III. Steven Green, his partner, warned him that this could be dangerous, but Watson ignored him.
   IV. A few minutes later, one of the bricks thrown by Watson smashed to the ground in front of an old man, who fainted out of fright.
   V. Mr. Watson began throwing some of the bricks over the side of the building.
   The MOST logical order for the above sentences to appear in the report is
   A. II, V, III, IV, I   B. I, IV, II, V, III   C. III, II, IV, V, I   D. II, III, I, IV, V

7. Police Officer Porter is completing an Incident Report concerning her rescue of a woman being held hostage by a former boyfriend. Her report will contain the following five sentences:
   I. I saw a man holding .25 caliber gun to a woman's head, but he did not see me.
   II. I then broke a window and gained access to the house.
   III. As I approached the house on foot, a gunshot rang out and I heard a woman scream.
   IV. A decoy van brought me as close as possible to the house where the woman was being held hostage.

V. I ordered the man to drop his gun, and he released the woman and was taken into custody.

The MOST logical order for the above sentences to appear in the report is
A. I, III, II, IV, V B. IV, III, II, I, V C. III, II, I, IV, V D. V, I, II, III, IV

8. Police Officer Byrnes is preparing a crime report concerning a robbery. The report will consist of the following five sentences:
   I. Mr. White, following the man's instructions, opened the car's hood, at which time the man got out of the auto, drew a revolver, and ordered White to give him all the money in his pockets.
   II. Investigation has determined there were no witnesses to this incident.
   III. The man asked White to check the oil and fill the tank.
   IV. Mr. White, a gas attendant, states that he was working alone at the gas station when a black male pulled up to the gas pump in a white Mercury.
   V. White was then bound and gagged by the male and locked in the gas station's rest room.

The MOST logical order for the above sentences to appear in the report is
A. IV, I, III, II, V B. III, I, II, V, IV C. IV, III, I, V, II D. I, III, IV, II, V

9. Police Officer Gale is preparing a report of a crime committed against Mr. Weston. The report will consist of the following five sentences:
   I. The man, who had a gun, told Mr. Weston not to scream for help and ordered him back into the apartment.
   II. With Mr. Weston disposed of in this fashion, the man proceeded to ransack the apartment.
   III. Opening the door to see who was there, Mr. Weston was confronted by a tall white male wearing a dark blue jacket and white pants.
   IV. Mr. Weston was at home alone in his living room when the doorbell rang.
   V. Once inside, the man bound and gagged Mr. Weston and locked him in the bathroom.

The MOST logical order for the above sentences to appear in the report is
A. III, V, II, I, IV B. IV, III, I, V, II C. III, V, IV, II, I D. IV, III, V, I, II

10. A police officer is completing a report of a robbery, which will contain the following five sentences:
    I. Two police officers were about to enter the Red Rose Coffee Shop on 47th Street and 8th Avenue.
    II. They then noticed a male running up the street carrying a brown paper bag.
    III. They heard a woman standing outside the Broadway Boutique yelling that her store had just been robbed by a young man, and she was pointing up the street.
    IV. They caught up with him and made an arrest.
    V. The police officers pursued the male, who ran past them on 8th Avenue.

The MOST logical order for the above sentences to appear in the report is
A. I, III, II, V, IV B. III, I, II, V, IV C. IV, V, I, II, III D. I, V, IV, III, II

11. Police Officer Capalbo is preparing a report of a bank robbery. The report will contain the following five statements made by a witness:
    I. Initialing, all I could see were two men, dressed in maintenance uniforms, sitting in the area reserved for bank officers.
    II. I was passing the bank at 8 P.M. and noticed that all the lights were out, except in the rear section.
    III. Then I noticed two other men in the bank, coming from the direction of the vault, carrying a large metal box.
    IV. At this point, I decided to call the police.
    V. I knocked on the window to get the attention of the men in the maintenance uniforms, and they chased the two men carrying the box down a flight of steps.

    The MOST logical order for the above sentences to appear in the report is
    A. IV, I, II, V, III B. I, III, II, V, IV C. II, I, III, V, IV D. II, III, I, V, IV

12. Police Officer Roberts is preparing a crime report concerning an assault and a stolen car. The report will contain the following five sentences:
    I. Upon leaving the store to return to his car, Winters noticed that a male unknown to him was sitting in his car.
    II. The man then re-entered Winters' car and drove away, fleeing north on 2nd Avenue.
    III. Mr. Winters stated that he parked his car in front of 235 East 25th Street and left the engine running while he went into the butcher shop at that location.
    IV. Mr. Robert Gering, a witness, stated that the male is known in the neighborhood as Bobby Rae and is believed to reside at 323 East 114th Street.
    V. When Winters approached the car and ordered the man to get out, the man got out of the auto and struck Winters with his fists, knocking him to the ground.

    The MOST logical order for the above sentences to appear in the report is
    A. III, II, V, I, IV B. III, I, V, II, IV C. I, IV, V, II, III D. III, II, I, V, IV

13. Police Officer Robinson is preparing a crime report concerning the robbery of Mr. Edwards' store. The report will consist of the following five sentences:
    I. When the last customer left the store, the two men drew revolvers and ordered Mr. Edwards to give them all the money in the cash register.
    II. The men proceeded to the back of the store as if they were going to do some shopping.
    III. Janet Morley, a neighborhood resident, later reported that she saw the men enter a green Ford station wagon and flee northbound on Albany Avenue.
    IV. Edwards complied after which the gunmen ran from the store.
    V. Mr. Edwards states that he was stocking merchandise behind the store counter when two white males entered the store.

    The MOST logical order for the above sentences to appear in the report is
    A. V, II, III, I, IV B. V, II, I, IV, III C. II, I, V, IV, III D. III, V, II, I, IV

14. Police Officer Wendell is preparing an accident report for a 6-car accident that occurred at the intersection of Bath Avenue and Bay Parkway. The report will consist of the following five sentences:
    I. A 2016 Volkswagen Beetle, traveling east on Bath Avenue, swerved to the left to avoid the Impala, and struck a 2014 Ford station wagon which was traveling west on Bath Avenue.
    II. The Seville then mounted the curb on the northeast corner of Bath Avenue and Bay Parkway and struck a light pole.
    III. A 2013 Buick Lesabre, traveling northbound on Bay Parkway directly behind the Impala, struck the Impala, pushing it into the intersection of Bath Avenue and Bay Parkway.
    IV. A 2015 Chevy Impala, traveling northbound on Bay Parkway, had stopped for a red light at Bath Avenue.
    V. A 2017 Toyota, traveling westbound on Bath Avenue, swerved to the right to avoid hitting the Ford station wagon, and struck a 2017 Cadillac Seville double-parked near the corner.
    The MOST logical order for the above sentences to appear in the report is
    A. IV, III, V, II, I B. III, IV, V, II, I C. IV, III, I, V, II D. III, IV, V, I, II

15. The following five sentences are part of an Activity Log entry Police Officer Rogers made regarding an explosion:
    I. I quickly treated the pedestrian for the injury.
    II. The explosion caused a glass window in an office building to shatter.
    III. After the pedestrian was treated, a call was placed to the precinct requesting additional police officers to evacuate the area.
    IV. After all the glass settled to the ground, I saw a pedestrian who was bleeding from the arm.
    V. While on foot patrol near 5th Avenue and 53rd Street, I heard a loud explosion.
    The MOST logical order for the above sentences to appear in the report is
    A. II, V, IV, I, III B. V, II, IV, III, I C. V, II, I, IV, III D. V, II, IV, I, III

16. Police Officer David is completing a report regarding illegal activity near the entrance to Madison Square Garden during a recent rock concert. The report will obtain the following five sentences:
    I. As I came closer to the man, he placed what appeared to be tickets in his pocket and began to walk away.
    II. After the man stopped, I questioned him about *scalping* tickets.
    III. While on assignment near the Madison Square Garden entrance, I observed a man apparently selling tickets.
    IV. I stopped the man by stating that I was a police officer.
    V. The man was then given a summons, and he left the area.
    The MOST logical order for the above sentences to appear in the report is
    A. I, III, IV, II, V B. III, I, IV, V, II C. III, IV, I, II, V D. III, I, IV, II, V

17. Police Officer Sampson is preparing a report containing a dispute in a bar. The report will contain the following five sentences:
   I. John Evans, the bartender, ordered the two men out of the bar.
   II. Two men dressed in dungarees entered the C and D Bar at 5:30 P.M.
   III. The two men refused to leave and began to beat up Evans.
   IV. A customer in the bar saw me on patrol and yelled to me to come separate the three men.
   V. The two men became very drunk and loud within a short time.
   The MOST logical order for the above sentences to appear in the report is
   A. II, I, V, III, IV   B. II, III, IV, V, I   C. III, I, II, V, IV   D. II, V, I, III, IV

18. A police officer is completing a report concerning the response to a crime in progress. The report will include the following five sentences:
   I. The officers saw two armed men run out of the liquor store and into a waiting car.
   II. Police Officers Lunty and Duren received the call and responded to the liquor store.
   III. The robbers gave up without a struggle.
   IV. Lunty and Duren blocked the getaway car with their patrol car.
   V. A call came into the precinct concerning a robbery in progress at Jane's Liquor Store.
   The MOST logical order for the above sentence to appear in the report is
   A. V, II, I, IV, III   B. II, V, I, III, IV   C. V, I, IV, II, III   D. I, V, II, III, IV

19. Police Officers Jenkins is preparing a Crime Report which will consist of the following five sentences:
   I. After making inquirie in the vicinity, Smith found out that his next door neighbor, Viola Jones, had seen two local teenagers, Michael Heinz and Vincent Gaynor, smash his car's windshields with a crowbar.
   II. Jones told Smith that the teenagers live at 8700 19th Avenue.
   III. Mr. Smith heard a loud crash at approximately 11:00 P.M., looked out of his apartment window, and saw two white males running away from his car.
   IV. Smith then reported the incident to the precinct, and Heinz and Gaynor were arrested at the address given.
   V. Leaving his apartment to investigate further, Smith discovered that his car's front and rear windshields had been smashed.
   The MOST logical order for the above sentences to appear in the report is
   A. III, IV, V, I, II   B. III, V, I, II, IV   C. III, I, V, II, IV   D. V, III, I, II, IV

20. Sergeant Nancy Winston is reviewing a Gun Control Report which will contain the following five sentences:
   I. The man fell to the floor when hit in the chest with three bullets from 22 caliber gun.
   II. Merriam's 22 caliber gun was seized, and he was given a summons for not having a pistol permit.
   III. Christopher Merriam, the owner of A-Z Grocery, shot a man who attempted to rob him.
   IV. Police Officer Franks responded and asked Merriam for his pistol permit, which he could not produce.

V. Merriam phoned the police to report he had just shot a man who had attempted to rob him.

The MOST logical order for the above sentences to appear in the report is
   A. III, I, V, IV, II   B. I, III, V, IV, II   C. III, I, V, II, IV   D. I, III, II, V, IV

21. Detective John Manville is completing a report for his superior regarding the murder of an unknown male who was shot in Central Park. The report will contain the following five sentences:
    I. Police Officers Langston and Cavers responded to the scene.
    II. I received the assignment to investigate the murder in Central Park from Detective Sergeant Rogers.
    III. Langston notified the Detective Bureau after questioning Jason.
    IV. An unknown male, apparently murdered, was discovered in Central Park by Howard Jason, a park employee, who immediately called the police.
    V. Langston and Cavers questioned Jason.

    The MOST logical order for the above sentences to appear in the report is
       A. I, IV, V, III, II   B. IV, I, V, II, III   C. IV, I, V, III, II   D. IV, V, I, III, II

22. A police officer is completing a report concerning the arrest of a juvenile. The report will contain the following five sentences:
    I. Sanders then telephoned Jay's parents from the precinct to inform them of their son's arrest.
    II. The store owner resisted, and Jay then shot him and ran from the store.
    III. Jay was transported directly to the precinct by Officer Sanders.
    IV. James Jay, a juvenile, walked into a candy store and announced a hold-up.
    V. Police Officer Sanders, while on patrol, arrested Jay a block from the candy store.

    The MOST logical order for the above sentences to appear in the report is
       A. IV, V, II, I, III   B. IV, II, V, III, I   C. II, IV, V, III, I   D. V, IV, II, I, III

23. Police Officer Olsen prepared a crime report for a robbery which contained the following five sentences:
    I. Mr. Gordon was approached by this individual who then produced a gun and demanded the money from the cash register.
    II. The man then fled from the scene on foot, southbound on 5th Avenue.
    III. Mr. Gordon was working at the deli counter when a white male, 5'6", 150-160 lbs., wearing a green jacket and blue pants, entered the store.
    IV. Mr. Gordon complied with the man's demands and handed him the daily receipts.
    V. Further investigation has determined there are no other witnesses to this robbery.

    The MOST logical order for the above sentences to appear in the report is
       A. I, III, IV, V, II   B. I, IV, II, III, V   C. III, IV, I, V, II   D. III, I, IV, II, V

24. Police Officer Bryant responded to 285 E. 31st Street to take a crime report of a burglary of Mr. Bond's home. The report will contain a brief description of the incident, consisting of the following five sentences:
   I. When Mr. Bond attempted to stop the burglar by grabbing him, he was pushed to the floor.
   II. The burglar had apparently gained access to the home by forcing open the 2nd floor bedroom window facing the fire escape.
   III. Mr. Bond sustained a head injury in the scuffle, and the burglar exited the home through the front door.
   IV. Finding nothing in the dresser, the burglar proceeded downstairs to the first floor, where he was confronted by Mr. Bond who was reading in the dining room.
   V. Once inside, he searched the drawers of the bedroom dresser.
   The MOST logical order for the above sentences to appear in the report is
      A. V, IV, I, II, III   B. II, V, IV, I, III   C. II, IV, V, III, I   D. III, II, I, V, IV

25. Police Officer Derringer responded to a call of a rape-homicide case in his patrol area and was ordered to prepare an incident report, which will contain the following five sentences:
   I. He pushed Miss Scott to the ground and forcibly raped her.
   II. Mary Scott was approached from behind by a white male, 5'7", 150-160 lbs. wearing dark pants and a white jacket.
   III. As Robinson approached the male, he ordered him to stop.
   IV. Screaming for help, Miss Scott alerted one John Robinson, a local grocer, who chased her assailant as he fled the scene.
   V. The male turned and fired two shots at Robinson, who fell to the ground mortally wounded.
   The MOST logical order for the above sentences to appear in the report is
      A. IV, III, I, II, V   B. II, IV, III, V, I   C. II, IV, I, V, III   D. II, I, IV, III, V

KEY (CORRECT ANSWERS)

1.	B		11.	C
2.	C		12.	B
3.	C		13.	B
4.	A		14.	C
5.	B		15.	D
6.	A		16.	D
7.	B		17.	D
8.	C		18.	A
9.	B		19.	B
10.	A		20.	A

21. C
22. B
23. D
24. B
25. D

PHILOSOPHY, PRINCIPLES, PRACTICES, AND TECHNICS OF SUPERVISION, ADMINISTRATION, MANAGEMENT, AND ORGANIZATION

TABLE OF CONTENTS

	Page
MEANING OF SUPERVISION	1
THE OLD AND THE NEW SUPERVISION	1
THE EIGHT (8) BASIC PRINCIPLES OF THE NEW SUPERVISION	1
I. Principle of Responsibility	1
II. Principle of Authority	2
III. Principle of Self-Growth	2
IV. Principle of Individual Worth	2
V. Principle of Creative Leadership	2
VI. Principle of Success and Failure	2
VII. Principle of Science	3
VIII. Principle of Cooperation	3
WHAT IS ADMINISTRATION?	3
I. Practices Commonly Classed as "Supervisory"	3
II. Practices Commonly Classed as "Administrative"	3
III. Practices Commonly Classed as Both "Supervisory" and "Administrative"	4
RESPONSIBILITIES OF THE SUPERVISOR	4
COMPETENCIES OF THE SUPERVISOR	4
THE PROFESSIONAL SUPERVISOR-EMPLOYEE RELATIONSHIP	4
MINI-TEXT IN SUPERVISION, ADMINISTRATION, MANAGEMENT, AND ORGANIZATION	5
I. Brief Highlights	5
A. Levels of Management	6
B. What the Supervisor Must Learn	6
C. A Definition of Supervision	6
D. Elements of the Team Concept	6
E. Principles of Organization	6
F. The Four Important Parts of Every Job	7
G. Principles of Delegation	7
H. Principles of Effective Communications	7
I. Principles of Work Improvement	7
J. Areas of Job Improvement	7
K. Seven Key Points in Making Improvements	8

L.	Corrective Techniques for Job Improvement	8
M.	A Planning Checklist	8
N.	Five Characteristics of Good Directions	9
O.	Types of Directions	9
P.	Controls	9
Q.	Orienting the New Employee	9
R.	Checklist for Orienting New Employees	9
S.	Principles of Learning	10
T.	Causes of Poor Performance	10
U.	Four Major Steps in On-the-Job Instructions	10
V.	Employees Want Five Things	10
W.	Some Don'ts in Regard to Praise	11
X.	How to Gain Your Workers' Confidence	11
Y.	Sources of Employee Problems	11
Z.	The Supervisor's Key to Discipline	11
AA.	Five Important Processes of Management	12
BB.	When the Supervisor Fails to Plan	12
CC.	Fourteen General Principles of Management	12
DD.	Change	12

II. Brief Topical Summaries — 13
   A. Who/What is the Supervisor? — 13
   B. The Sociology of Work — 13
   C. Principles and Practices of Supervision — 14
   D. Dynamic Leadership — 14
   E. Processes for Solving Problems — 15
   F. Training for Results — 15
   G. Health, Safety, and Accident Prevention — 16
   H. Equal Employment Opportunity — 16
   I. Improving Communications — 16
   J. Self-Development — 17
   K. Teaching and Training — 17
      1. The Teaching Process — 17
         a. Preparation — 17
         b. Presentation — 18
         c. Summary — 18
         d. Application — 18
         e. Evaluation — 18
      2. Teaching Methods — 18
         a. Lecture — 18
         b. Discussion — 18
         c. Demonstration — 19
         d. Performance — 19
         e. Which Method to Use — 19

PHILOSOPHY, PRINCIPLES, PRACTICES, AND TECHNICS
OF
SUPERVISION, ADMINISTRATION, MANAGEMENT, AND ORGANIZATION

MEANING OF SUPERVISION

The extension of the democratic philosophy has been accompanied by an extension in the scope of supervision. Modern leaders and supervisors no longer think of supervision in the narrow sense of being confined chiefly to visiting employees, supplying materials, or rating the staff. They regard supervision as being intimately related to all the concerned agencies of society, they speak of the supervisor's function in terms of "growth," rather than the "improvement" of employees.

This modern concept of supervision may be defined as follows: Supervision is leadership and the development of leadership within groups which are cooperatively engaged in inspection, research, training, guidance, and evaluation.

THE OLD AND THE NEW SUPERVISION

TRADITIONAL
1. Inspection
2. Focused on the employee
3. Visitation
4. Random and haphazard
5. Imposed and authoritarian
6. One person usually

MODERN
1. Study and analysis
2. Focused on aims, materials, methods, supervisors, employees, environment
3. Demonstrations, intervisitation, workshops, directed reading, bulletins, etc.
4. Definitely organized and planned (scientific)
5. Cooperative and democratic
6. Many persons involved (creative)

THE EIGHT (8) BASIC PRINCIPLES OF THE NEW SUPERVISION

I. Principle of Responsibility
   Authority to act and responsibility for acting must be joined.
   A. If you give responsibility, give authority.
   B. Define employee duties clearly.
   C. Protect employees from criticism by others.
   D. Recognize the rights as well as obligations of employees.
   E. Achieve the aims of a democratic society insofar as it is possible within the area of your work.
   F. Establish a situation favorable to training and learning.
   G. Accept ultimate responsibility for everything done in your section, unit, office, division, department.
   H. Good administration and good supervision are inseparable.

II. Principle of Authority
The success of the supervisor is measured by the extent to which the power of authority is not used.
   A. Exercise simplicity and informality in supervision
   B. Use the simplest machinery of supervision
   C. If it is good for the organization as a whole, it is probably justified.
   D. Seldom be arbitrary or authoritative.
   E. Do not base your work on the power of position or of personality.
   F. Permit and encourage the free expression of opinions.

III. Principle of Self-Growth
The success of the supervisor is measured by the extent to which, and the speed with which, he is no longer needed.
   A. Base criticism on principles, not on specifics.
   B. Point out higher activities to employees.
   C. Train for self-thinking by employees to meet new situations.
   D. Stimulate initiative, self-reliance, and individual responsibility
   E. Concentrate on stimulating the growth of employees rather than on removing defects.

IV. Principle of Individual Worth
Respect for the individual is a paramount consideration in supervision.
   A. Be human and sympathetic in dealing with employees.
   B. Don't nag about things to be done.
   C. Recognize the individual differences among employees and seek opportunities to permit best expression of each personality.

V. Principle of Creative Leadership
The best supervision is that which is not apparent to the employee.
   A. Stimulate, don't drive employees to creative action.
   B. Emphasize doing good things.
   C. Encourage employees to do what they do best.
   D. Do not be too greatly concerned with details of subject or method.
   E. Do not be concerned exclusively with immediate problems and activities.
   F. Reveal higher activities and make them both desired and maximally possible.
   G. Determine procedures in the light of each situation but see that these are derived from a sound basic philosophy.
   H. Aid, inspire, and lead so as to liberate the creative spirit latent in all good employees.

VI. Principle of Success and Failure
There are no unsuccessful employees, only unsuccessful supervisors who have failed to give proper leadership.
   A. Adapt suggestions to the capacities, attitudes, and prejudices of employees.
   B. Be gradual, be progressive, be persistent.
   C. Help the employee find the general principle; have the employee apply his own problem to the general principle.
   D. Give adequate appreciation for good work and honest effort.
   E. Anticipate employee difficulties and help to prevent them.
   F. Encourage employees to do the desirable things they will do anyway.
   G. Judge your supervision by the results it secures.

VII. Principle of Science
Successful supervision is scientific, objective, and experimental. It is based on facts, not on prejudices.
   A. Be cumulative in results.
   B. Never divorce your suggestions from the goals of training.
   C. Don't be impatient of results.
   D. Keep all matters on a professional, not a personal, level.
   E. Do not be concerned exclusively with immediate problems and activities.
   F. Use objective means of determining achievement and rating where possible.

VIII. Principle of Cooperation
Supervision is a cooperative enterprise between supervisor and employee.
   A. Begin with conditions as they are.
   B. Ask opinions of all involved when formulating policies.
   C. Organization is as good as its weakest link.
   D. Let employees help to determine policies and department programs.
   E. Be approachable and accessible—physically and mentally.
   F. Develop pleasant social relationships.

WHAT IS ADMINISTRATION

Administration is concerned with providing the environment, the material facilities, and the operational procedures that will promote the maximum growth and development of supervisors and employees. (Organization is an aspect and a concomitant of administration.)

There is no sharp line of demarcation between supervision and administration; these functions are intimately interrelated and, often, overlapping. They are complementary activities.

I. Practices Commonly Classed as "Supervisory"
   A. Conducting employees' conferences
   B. Visiting sections, units, offices, divisions, departments
   C. Arranging for demonstrations
   D. Examining plans
   E. Suggesting professional reading
   F. Interpreting bulletins
   G. Recommending in-service training courses
   H. Encouraging experimentation
   I. Appraising employee morale
   J. Providing for intervisitation

II. Practices Commonly Classified as "Administrative"
   A. Management of the office
   B. Arrangement of schedules for extra duties
   C. Assignment of rooms or areas
   D. Distribution of supplies
   E. Keeping records and reports
   F. Care of audio-visual materials
   G. Keeping inventory records
   H. Checking record cards and books

    I. Programming special activities
    J. Checking on the attendance and punctuality of employees

III. Practices Commonly Classified as Both "Supervisory" and "Administrative"
    A. Program construction
    B. Testing or evaluating outcomes
    C. Personnel accounting
    D. Ordering instructional materials

RESPONSIBILITIES OF THE SUPERVISOR

A person employed in a supervisory capacity must constantly be able to improve his own efficiency and ability. He represent the employer to the employees and only continuous self-examination can make him a capable supervisor.

Leadership and training are the supervisor's responsibility. An efficient working unit is one in which the employees work with the supervisor. It is his job to bring out the best in his employees. He must always be relaxed, courteous, and calm in his association with his employees. Their feelings are important, and a harsh attitude does not develop the most efficient employees.

COMPETENCES OF THE SUPERVISOR

    I. Complete knowledge of the duties and responsibilities of his position.
    II. To be able to organize a job, plan ahead, and carry through.
    III. To have self-confidence and initiative.
    IV. To be able to handle the unexpected situation and make quick decisions.
    V. To be able to properly train subordinates in the positions they are best suited for.
    VI. To be able to keep good human relations among his subordinates.
    VII. To be able to keep good human relations between his subordinates and himself and to earn their respect and trust.

THE PROFESSIONAL SUPERVISOR-EMPLOYEE RELATIONSHIP

There are two kinds of efficiency: one kind is only apparent and is produced in organizations through the exercise of mere discipline; this is but a simulation of the second, or true, efficiency which springs from spontaneous cooperation. If you are a manager, no matter how great or small your responsibility, it is your job, in the final analysis, to create and develop this involuntary cooperation among the people whom you supervise. For, no matter how powerful a combination of money, machines, and materials a company may have, this is a dead and sterile thing without a team of willing, thinking, and articulate people to guide it.

The following 21 points are presented as indicative of the exemplary basic relationship that should exist between supervisor and employee:

1. Each person wants to be liked and respected by his fellow employee and wants to be treated with consideration and respect by his superior.
2. The most competent employee will make an error. However, in a unit where good relations exist between the supervisor and his employees, tenseness and fear do not exist. Thus, errors are not hidden or covered up, and the efficiency of a unit is not impaired.

3. Subordinates resent rules, regulations, or orders that are unreasonable or unexplained.
4. Subordinates are quick to resent unfairness, harshness, injustices, and favoritism.
5. An employee will accept responsibility if he knows that he will be complimented for a job well done, and not too harshly chastised for failure; that his supervisor will check the cause of the failure, and, if it was the supervisor's fault, he will assume the blame therefore. If it was the employee's fault, his supervisor will explain the correct method or means of handling the responsibility.
6. An employee wants to receive credit for a suggestion he has made, that is used. If a suggestion cannot be used, the employee is entitled to an explanation. The supervisor should not say "no" and close the subject.
7. Fear and worry slow up a worker's ability. Poor working environment can impair his physical and mental health. A good supervisor avoids forceful methods, threats, and arguments to get a job done.
8. A forceful supervisor is able to train his employees individually and as a team, and is able to motivate them in the proper channels.
9. A mature supervisor is able to properly evaluate his subordinates and to keep them happy and satisfied.
10. A sensitive supervisor will never patronize his subordinates.
11. A worthy supervisor will respect his employees' confidences.
12. Definite and clear-cut responsibilities should be assigned to each executive.
13. Responsibility should always be coupled with corresponding authority.
14. No change should be made in the scope or responsibilities of a position without a definite understanding to that effect on the part of all persons concerned.
15. No executive or employee, occupying a single position in the organization, should be subject to definite orders from more than one source.
16. Orders should never be given to subordinates over the head of a responsible executive. Rather than do this, the officer in question should be supplanted.
17. Criticisms of subordinates should, whoever possible, be made privately, and in no case should a subordinate be criticized in the presence of executives or employees of equal or lower rank.
18. No dispute or difference between executives or employees as to authority or responsibilities should be considered too trivial for prompt and careful adjudication.
19. Promotions, wage changes, and disciplinary action should always be approved by the executive immediately superior to the one directly responsible.
20. No executive or employee should ever be required, or expected, to be at the same time an assistant to, and critic of, another.
21. Any executive whose work is subject to regular inspection should, wherever practicable, be given the assistance and facilities necessary to enable him to maintain an independent check of the quality of his work.

MINI-TEXT IN SUPERVISION, ADMINISTRATION, MANAGEMENT, AND ORGANIZATION

I. Brief Highlights

Listed concisely and sequentially are major headings and important data in the field for quick recall and review.

A. Levels of Management
Any organization of some size has several levels of management. In terms of a ladder, the levels are:

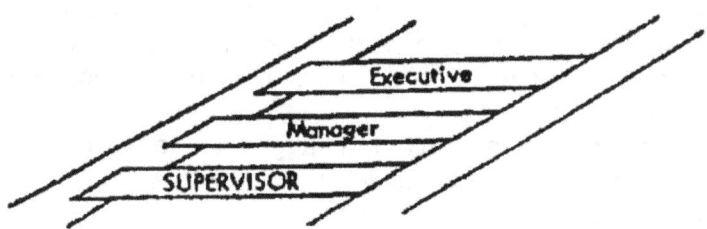

The first level is very important because it is the beginning point of management leadership.

B. What the Supervisor Must Learn
A supervisor must learn to:
1. Deal with people and their differences
2. Get the job done through people
3. Recognize the problems when they exist
4. Overcome obstacles to good performance
5. Evaluate the performance of people
6. Check his own performance in terms of accomplishment

C. A Definition of Supervisor
The term supervisor means any individual having authority, in the interests of the employer, to hire, transfer, suspend, lay-off, recall, promote, discharge, assign, reward, or discipline other employees or responsibility to direct them, or to adjust their grievances, or effectively to recommend such action, if, in connection with the foregoing, exercise of such authority is not of a merely routine or clerical nature but requires the use of independent judgment.

D. Elements of the Team Concept
What is involved in teamwork? The component parts are:
1. Members
2. A leader
3. Goals
4. Plans
5. Cooperation
6. Spirit

E. Principles of Organization
1. A team member must know what his job is.
2. Be sure that the nature and scope of a job are understood.
3. Authority and responsibility should be carefully spelled out.
4. A supervisor should be permitted to make the maximum number of decisions affecting his employees.
5. Employees should report to only one supervisor.
6. A supervisor should direct only as many employees as he can handle effectively.
7. An organization plan should be flexible.

8. Inspection and performance of work should be separate.
9. Organizational problems should receive immediate attention.
10. Assign work in line with ability and experience.

F. The Four Important Parts of Every Job
1. Inherent in every job is the *accountability* for results.
2. A second set of factors in every job is *responsibilities*.
3. Along with duties and responsibilities one must have the *authority* to act within certain limits without obtaining permission to proceed.
4. No job exists in a vacuum. The supervisor is surrounded by key *relationships*.

G. Principles of Delegation
Where work is delegated for the first time, the supervisor should think in terms of these questions:
1. Who is best qualified to do this?
2. Can an employee improve his abilities by doing this?
3. How long should an employee spend on this?
4. Are there any special problems for which he will need guidance?
5. How broad a delegation can I make?

H. Principles of Effective Communications
1. Determine the media.
2. To whom directed?
3. Identification and source authority.
4. Is communication understood?

I. Principles of Work Improvement
1. Most people usually do only the work which is assigned to them.
2. Workers are likely to fit assigned work into the time available to perform it.
3. A good workload usually stimulates output.
4. People usually do their best work when they know that results will be reviewed or inspected.
5. Employees usually feel that someone else is responsible for conditions of work, workplace layout, job methods, type of tools/equipment, and other such factors.
6. Employees are usually defensive about their job security.
7. Employees have natural resistance to change.
8. Employees can support or destroy a supervisor.
9. A supervisor usually earns the respect of his people through his personal example of diligence and efficiency.

J. Areas of Job Improvement
The areas of job improvement are quite numerous, but the most common ones which a supervisor can identify and utilize are:
1. Departmental layout
2. Flow of work
3. Workplace layout
4. Utilization of manpower
5. Work methods
6. Materials handling

7. Utilization
8. Motion economy

K. Seven Key Points in Making Improvements
1. Select the job to be improved
2. Study how it is being done now
3. Question the present method
4. Determine actions to be taken
5. Chart proposed method
6. Get approval and apply
7. Solicit worker participation

I. Corrective Techniques of Job Improvement
Specific Problems
1. Size of workload
2. Inability to meet schedules
3. Strain and fatigue
4. Improper use of men and skills
5. Waste, poor quality, unsafe conditions
6. Bottleneck conditions that hinder output
7. Poor utilization of equipment and machine
8. Efficiency and productivity of labor

General Improvement
1. Departmental layout
2. Flow of work
3. Work plan layout
4. Utilization of manpower
5. Work methods
6. Materials handling
7. Utilization of equipment
8. Motion economy

Corrective Techniques
1. Study with scale model
2. Flow chart study
3. Motion analysis
4. Comparison of units produced to standard allowance
5. Methods analysis
6. Flow chart and equipment study
7. Down time vs. running time
8. Motion analysis

M. A Planning Checklist
1. Objectives
2. Controls
3. Delegations
4. Communications
5. Resources
6. Manpower

7. Equipment
8. Supplies and materials
9. Utilization of time
10. Safety
11. Money
12. Work
13. Timing of improvements

N. Five Characteristics of Good Directions
In order to get results, directions must be:
1. Possible of accomplishment
2. Agreeable with worker interests
3. Related to mission
4. Planned and complete
5. Unmistakably clear

O. Types of Directions
1. Demands or direct orders
2. Requests
3. Suggestion or implication
4. volunteering

P. Controls
A typical listing of the overall areas in which the supervisor should establish controls might be:
1. Manpower
2. Materials
3. Quality of work
4. Quantity of work
5. Time
6. Space
7. Money
8. Methods

Q. Orienting the New Employee
1. Prepare for him
2. Welcome the new employee
3. Orientation for the job
4. Follow-up

R. Checklist for Orienting New Employees   Yes   No
1. Do you appreciate the feelings of new employees
   when they first report for work?   ___   ___
2. Are you aware of the fact that the new employee must
   make a big adjustment to his job?   ___   ___
3. Have you given him good reasons for liking the job and
   the organization?   ___   ___
4. Have you prepared for his first day on the job?   ___   ___
5. Did you welcome him cordially and make him feel needed?   ___   ___

	Yes	No

6. Did you establish rapport with him so that he feels free to talk and discuss matters with you?
7. Did you explain his job to him and his relationship to you?
8. Does he know that his work will be evaluated periodically on a basis that is fair and objective?
9. Did you introduce him to his fellow workers in such a way that they are likely to accept him?
10. Does he know what employee benefits he will receive?
11. Does he understand the importance of being on the job and what to do if he must leave his duty station?
12. Has he been impressed with the importance of accident prevention and safe practice?
13. Does he generally know his way around the department?
14. Is he under the guidance of a sponsor who will teach the right way of doing things?
15. Do you plan to follow-up so that he will continue to adjust successfully to his job?

S. Principles of Learning
   1. Motivation
   2. Demonstration or explanation
   3. Practice

T. Causes of Poor Performance
   1. Improper training for job
   2. Wrong tools
   3. Inadequate directions
   4. Lack of supervisory follow-up
   5. Poor communications
   6. Lack of standards of performance
   7. Wrong work habits
   8. Low morale
   9. Other

U. Four Major Steps in On-The-Job Instruction
   1. Prepare the worker
   2. Present the operation
   3. Tryout performance
   4. Follow-up

V. Employees Want Five Things
   1. Security
   2. Opportunity
   3. Recognition
   4. Inclusion
   5. Expression

W. Some Don'ts in Regard to Praise
1. Don't praise a person for something he hasn't done.
2. Don't praise a person unless you can be sincere.
3. Don't be sparing in praise just because your superior withholds it from you.
4. Don't let too much time elapse between good performance and recognition of it

X. How to Gain Your Workers' Confidence
Methods of developing confidence include such things as:
1. Knowing the interests, habits, hobbies of employees
2. Admitting your own inadequacies
3. Sharing and telling of confidence in others
4. Supporting people when they are in trouble
5. Delegating matters that can be well handled
6. Being frank and straightforward about problems and working conditions
7. Encouraging others to bring their problems to you
8. Taking action on problems which impede worker progress

Y. Sources of Employee Problems
On-the-job causes might be such things as:
1. A feeling that favoritism is exercised in assignments
2. Assignment of overtime
3. An undue amount of supervision
4. Changing methods or systems
5. Stealing of ideas or trade secrets
6. Lack of interest in job
7. Threat of reduction in force
8. Ignorance or lack of communications
9. Poor equipment
10. Lack of knowing how supervisor feels toward employee
11. Shift assignments

Off-the-job problems might have to do with:
1. Health
2. Finances
3. Housing
4. Family

Z. The Supervisor's Key to Discipline
There are several key points about discipline which the supervisor should keep in mind:
1. Job discipline is one of the disciplines of life and is directed by the supervisor.
2. It is more important to correct an employee fault than to fix blame for it.
3. Employee performance is affected by problems both on the job and off.
4. Sudden or abrupt changes in behavior can be indications of important employee problems.
5. Problems should be dealt with as soon as possible after they are identified.
6. The attitude of the supervisor may have more to do with solving problems than the techniques of problem solving.
7. Correction of employee behavior should be resorted to only after the supervisor is sure that training or counseling will not be helpful.

8. Be sure to document your disciplinary actions.
9. Make sure that you are disciplining on the basis of facts rather than personal feelings.
10. Take each disciplinary step in order, being careful not to make snap judgments, or decisions based on impatience.

AA. Five Important Processes of Management
1. Planning
2. Organizing
3. Scheduling
4. Controlling
5. Motivating

BB. When the Supervisor Fails to Plan
1. Supervisor creates impression of not knowing his job
2. May lead to excessive overtime
3. Job runs itself—supervisor lacks control
4. Deadlines and appointments missed
5. Parts of the work go undone
6. Work interrupted by emergencies
7. Sets a bad example
8. Uneven workload creates peaks and valleys
9. Too much time on minor details at expense of more important tasks

CC. Fourteen General Principles of Management
1. Division of work
2. Authority and responsibility
3. Discipline
4. Unity of command
5. Unity of direction
6. Subordination of individual interest to general interest
7. Remuneration of personnel
8. Centralization
9. Scalar chain
10. Order
11. Equity
12. Stability of tenure of personnel
13. Initiative
14. Esprit de corps

DD. Change

Bringing about change is perhaps attempted more often, and yet less well understood, than anything else the supervisor does. How do people generally react to change? (People tend to resist change that is imposed upon them by other individuals or circumstances.

Change is characteristic of every situation. It is a part of every real endeavor where the efforts of people are concerned.

1. Why do people resist change?
   People may resist change because of:
   a. Fear of the unknown
   b. Implied criticism
   c. Unpleasant experiences in the past
   d. Fear of loss of status
   e. Threat to the ego
   f. Fear of loss of economic stability

2. How can we best overcome the resistance to change?
   In initiating change, take these steps:
   a. Get ready to sell
   b. Identify sources of help
   c. Anticipate objections
   d. Sell benefits
   e. Listen in depth
   f. Follow up

II. Brief Topical Summaries

   A. Who/What is the Supervisor?
      1. The supervisor is often called the "highest level employee and the lowest level manager."
      2. A supervisor is a member of both management and the work group. He acts as a bridge between the two.
      3. Most problems in supervision are in the area of human relations, or people problems.
      4. Employees expect: Respect, opportunity to learn and to advance, and a sense of belonging, and so forth.
      5. Supervisors are responsible for directing people and organizing work. Planning is of paramount importance.
      6. A position description is a set of duties and responsibilities inherent to a given position.
      7. It is important to keep the position description up-to-date and to provide each employee with his own copy.

   B. The Sociology of Work
      1. People are alike in many ways; however, each individual is unique.
      2. The supervisor is challenged in getting to know employee differences. Acquiring skills in evaluating individuals is an asset.
      3. Maintaining meaningful working relationships in the organization is of great importance.
      4. The supervisor has an obligation to help individuals to develop to their fullest potential.
      5. Job rotation on a planned basis helps to build versatility and to maintain interest and enthusiasm in work groups.
      6. Cross training (job rotation) provides backup skills.

7. The supervisor can help reduce tension by maintaining a sense of humor, providing guidance to employees, and by making reasonable and timely decisions. Employees respond favorably to working under reasonably predictable circumstances.
8. Change is characteristic of all managerial behavior. The supervisor must adjust to changes in procedures, new methods, technological changes, and to a number of new and sometimes challenging situations.
9. To overcome the natural tendency for people to resist change, the supervisor should become more skillful in initiating change.

C. Principles and Practices of Supervision
1. Employees should be required to answer to only one superior.
2. A supervisor can effectively direct only a limited number of employees, depending upon the complexity, variety, and proximity of the jobs involved.
3. The organizational chart presents the organization in graphic form. It reflects lines of authority and responsibility as well as interrelationships of units within the organization.
4. Distribution of work can be improved through an analysis using the "Work Distribution Chart."
5. The "Work Distribution Chart" reflects the division of work within a unit in understandable form.
6. When related tasks are given to an employee, he has a better chance of increasing his skills through training.
7. The individual who is given the responsibility for tasks must also be given the appropriate authority to insure adequate results.
8. The supervisor should delegate repetitive, routine work. Preparation of recurring reports, maintaining leave and attendance records are some examples.
9. Good discipline is essential to good task performance. Discipline is reflected in the actions of employees on the job in the absence of supervision.
10. Disciplinary action may have to be taken when the positive aspects of discipline have failed. Reprimand, warning, and suspension are examples of disciplinary action.
11. If a situation calls for a reprimand, be sure it is deserved and remember it is to be done in private.

D. Dynamic Leadership
1. A style is a personal method or manner of exerting influence.
2. Authoritarian leaders often see themselves as the source of power and authority.
3. The democratic leader often perceives the group as the source of authority and power.
4. Supervisors tend to do better when using the pattern of leadership that is most natural for them.
5. Social scientists suggest that the effective supervisor use the leadership style that best fits the problem or circumstances involved.
6. All four styles—telling, selling, consulting, joining—have their place. Using one does not preclude using the other at another time.

7. The theory X point of view assumes that the average person dislikes work, will avoid it whenever possible, and must be coerced to achieve organizational objectives.
8. The theory Y point of view assumes that the average person considers work to be a natural as play, and, when the individual is committed, he requires little supervision or direction to accomplish desired objectives.
9. The leader's basic assumptions concerning human behavior and human nature affect his actions, decisions, and other managerial practices.
10. Dissatisfaction among employees is often present, but difficult to isolate. The supervisor should seek to weaken dissatisfaction by keeping promises, being sincere and considerate, keeping employees informed, and so forth.
11. Constructive suggestions should be encouraged during the natural progress of the work.

E. Processes for Solving Problems
1. People find their daily tasks more meaningful and satisfying when they can improve them.
2. The causes of problems, or the key factors, are often hidden in the background. Ability to solve problems often involves the ability to isolate them from their backgrounds. There is some substance to the cliché that some persons "can't see the forest for the trees."
3. New procedures are often developed from old ones. Problems should be broken down into manageable parts. New ideas can be adapted from old one.
4. People think differently in problem-solving situations. Using a logical, patterned approach is often useful. One approach found to be useful includes these steps:
   a. Define the problem
   b. Establish objectives
   c. Get the facts
   d. Weigh and decide
   e. Take action
   f. Evaluate action

F. Training for Results
1. Participants respond best when they feel training is important to them.
2. The supervisor has responsibility for the training and development of those who report to him.
3. When training is delegated to others, great care must be exercised to insure the trainer has knowledge, aptitude, and interest for his work as a trainer.
4. Training (learning) of some type goes on continually. The most successful supervisor makes certain the learning contributes in a productive manner to operational goals.
5. New employees are particularly susceptible to training. Older employees facing new job situations require specific training, as well as having need for development and growth opportunities.
6. Training needs require continuous monitoring.
7. The training officer of an agency is a professional with a responsibility to assist supervisors in solving training problems.

8. Many of the self-development steps important to the supervisor's own growth are equally important to the development of peers and subordinates. Knowledge of these is important when the supervisor consults with others on development and growth opportunities.

G. Health, Safety, and Accident Prevention
1. Management-minded supervisors take appropriate measures to assist employees in maintaining health and in assuring safe practices in the work environment.
2. Effective safety training and practices help to avoid injury and accidents.
3. Safety should be a management goal. All infractions of safety which are observed should be corrected without exception.
4. Employees' safety attitude, training and instruction, provision of safe tools and equipment, supervision, and leadership are considered highly important factors which contribute to safety and which can be influenced directly by supervisors.
5. When accidents do occur, they should be investigated promptly for very important reasons, including the fact that information which is gained can be used to prevent accidents in the future.

H. Equal Employment Opportunity
1. The supervisor should endeavor to treat all employees fairly, without regard to religion, race, sex, or national origin.
2. Groups tend to reflect the attitude of the leader. Prejudice can be detected even in very subtle form. Supervisors must strive to create a feeling of mutual respect and confidence in every employee.
3. Complete utilization of all human resources is a national goal. Equitable consideration should be accorded women in the work force, minority-group members, the physically and mentally handicapped, and the older employee. The important question is: "Who can do the job?"
4. Training opportunities, recognition for performance, overtime assignments, promotional opportunities, and all other personnel actions are to be handled on an equitable basis.

I. Improving Communications
1. Communications is achieving understanding between the sender and the receiver of a message. It also means sharing information—the creation of understanding.
2. Communication is basic to all human activity. Words are means of conveying meanings; however, real meanings are in people.
3. There are very practical differences in the effectiveness of one-way, impersonal, and two-way communications. Words spoken face-to-face are better understood. Telephone conversations are effective, but lack the rapport of person-to-person exchanges. The whole person communicates.
4. Cooperation and communication in an organization go hand in hand. When there is a mutual respect between people, spelling out rules and procedures for communicating is unnecessary.
5. There are several barriers to effective communications. These include failure to listen with respect and understanding, lack of skill in feedback, and misinterpreting the meanings of words used by the speaker. It is also common

practice to listen to what we want to hear, and tune out things we do not want to hear.
6. Communication is management's chief problem. The supervisor should accept the challenge to communicate more effectively and to improve interagency and intra-agency communications.
7. The supervisor may often plan for and conduct meetings. The planning phase is critical and may determine the success or the failure of a meeting.
8. Speaking before groups usually requires extra effort. Stage fright may never disappear completely, but it can be controlled.

J. Self-Development
1. Every employee is responsible for his own self-development.
2. Toastmaster and toastmistress clubs offer opportunities to improve skills in oral communications.
3. Planning for one's own self-development is of vital importance. Supervisors know their own strengths and limitations better than anyone else.
4. Many opportunities are open to aid the supervisor in his developmental efforts, including job assignments; training opportunities, both governmental and non-governmental—to include universities and professional conferences and seminars.
5. Programmed instruction offers a means of studying at one's own rate.
6. Where difficulties may arise from a supervisor's being away from his work for training, he may participate in televised home study or correspondence courses to meet his self-development needs.

K. Teaching and Training
1. The Teaching Process
Teaching is encouraging and guiding the learning activities of students toward established goals. In most cases this process consists of five steps: preparation, presentation, summarization, evaluation, and application.

   a. Preparation
   Preparation is two-fold in nature; that of the supervisor and the employee. Preparation by the supervisor is absolutely essential to success. He must know what, when, where, how, and whom he will teach. Some of the factors that should be considered are:
   1) The objectives
   2) The materials needed
   3) The methods to be used
   4) Employee participation
   5) Employee interest
   6) Training aids
   7) Evaluation
   8) Summarization

   Employee preparation consists in preparing the employee to receive the material. Probably the most important single factor in the preparation of the employee is arousing and maintaining his interest. He must know the objectives of the training, why he is there, how the material can be used, and its importance to him.

b. Presentation
In presentation, have a carefully designed plan and follow it. The plan should be accurate and complete, yet flexible enough to meet situations as they arise. The method of presentation will be determined by the particular situation and objectives.

c. Summary
A summary should be made at the end of every training unit and program. In addition, there may be internal summaries depending on the nature of the material being taught. The important thing is that the trainee must always be able to understand how each part of the new material relates to the whole.

d. Application
The supervisor must arrange work so the employee will be given a chance to apply new knowledge or skills while the material is still clear in his mind and interest is high. The trainee does not really know whether he has learned the material until he has been given a chance to apply it. If the material is not applied, it loses most of its value.

e. Evaluation
The purpose of all training is to promote learning. To determine whether the training has been a success or failure, the supervisor must evaluate this learning.
In the broadest sense, evaluation includes all the devices, methods, skills, and techniques used by the supervisor to keep himself and the employees informed as to their progress toward the objectives they are pursuing. The extent to which the employee has mastered the knowledge, skills, and abilities, or changed his attitudes, as determined by the program objectives, is the extent to which instruction has succeeded or failed.
Evaluation should not be confined to the end of the lesson, day, or program but should be used continuously. We shall note later the way this relates to the rest of the teaching process.

2. Teaching Methods
A teaching method is a pattern of identifiable student and instructor activity used in presenting training material.
All supervisors are faced with the problem of deciding which method should be used at a given time.

a. Lecture
The lecture is direct oral presentation of material by the supervisor. The present trend is to place less emphasis on the trainer's activity and more on that of the trainee.

b. Discussion
Teaching by discussion or conference involves using questions and other techniques to arouse interest and focus attention upon certain areas, and by doing so creating a learning situation. This can be one of the most

valuable methods because it gives the employees an opportunity to express their ideas and pool their knowledge.

    c. Demonstration
The demonstration is used to teach how something works or how to do something. It can be used to show a principle or what the results of a series of actions will be. A well-staged demonstration is particularly effective because it shows proper methods of performance in a realistic manner.

    d. Performance
Performance is one of the most fundamental of all learning techniques or teaching methods. The trainee may be able to tell how a specific operation should be performed but he cannot be sure he knows how to perform the operation until he has done so.
As with all methods, there are certain advantages and disadvantages to each method.

    e. Which Method to Use
Moreover, there are other methods and techniques of teaching. It is difficult to use any method without other methods entering into it. In any learning situation, a combination of methods is usually more effective than any one method alone.

Finally, evaluation must be integrated into the other aspects of the teaching-learning process.

It must be used in the motivation of the trainees; it must be used to assist in developing understanding during the training; and it must be related to employee application of the results of training.

This is distinctly the role of the supervisor.

www.ingramcontent.com/pod-product-compliance
Lightning Source LLC
Chambersburg PA
CBHW080321020526
44117CB00035B/2588